HEALING CRYSTALS

Beginner's Guide to Understanding the Healing Power of Crystals and Healing Stones

Crystal Lee

© Copyright 2018 by Crystal Lee – All rights reserved.

No part of this book may be reproduced or transmitted in any form or by any means, electronic or mechanical, including photocopying, recording or by any information storage and retrieval system without written permission of the publisher, except for the inclusion of brief quotations in a review.

The following eBook is reproduced below with the goal of providing information that is as accurate and reliable as possible. Regardless, purchasing this eBook can be seen as consent to the fact that both the publisher and the author of this book is in no way experts on the topics discussed within and that any recommendations or suggestions that are made herein are for entertainment purposes only. Professionals should be consulted as needed prior to undertaking any of the actions endorsed herein.

This declaration is deemed fair and valid by both the American Bar Association and the Committee of Publishers Association and is legally binding throughout the United States.

Furthermore, the transmission, duplication or reproduction of any of the following work including specific information will be considered an illegal act irrespective of whether it is done electronically or in print. This extends to creating a secondary or tertiary copy of the work or a recorded copy and is only allowed with express written consent from the Publisher. All additional rights reserved.

The information in the following pages is broadly considered to be a truthful and accurate account of facts and as such any inattention, use or misuse of the information in question by the reader will render any resulting actions solely under their purview. There are no scenarios in which the publisher or the original author of this work can be in any fashion deemed liable for any hardship or damages that may befall them after undertaking information described herein.

Additionally, the information in the following pages is intended only for informational purposes and should thus be thought of as universal. As befitting its nature, it is presented without assurance regarding its prolonged validity or interim quality. Trademarks that are mentioned are done without written consent and can in no way be considered an endorsement from the trademark holder.

TABLE OF CONTENTS

Introduction 1
Chapter 1 *Properties And Powers Of Crystals* 2
Chapter 2 *Crystals And Healing* 29
Chapter 3 *Creating Crystal Grids* 41
Chapter 4 *Crystals And Chakras* 47
Chapter 5 *Crystals In Reiki* 53
Chapter 6 *Clearing And Protection With Crystals* 55
Chapter 7 *Using Crystals For Holistic Living* 60
Chapter 8 *Crystals For Disorders, Specific Ailments, And Systems* 82
Conclusion 89
Description 90

INTRODUCTION

Congratulations on downloading your copy of *Healing Crystals: The Beginner's Guide to Understanding the Healing Power of Crystals and Healing Stones*. I am so glad you have decided to explore the healing power of crystals to help create positive changes in your life. You will soon discover the properties and healing powers of many crystals, how to use specific crystals to heal the body, mind, and spirit and how to create crystal grids. The following chapters will also discuss chakra balancing using crystals, crystals in Reiki sessions, utilizing crystals to clear negativity while attracting unconditional love, practicing crystal healing in all aspects of your life including relaxation, centering, meditation, and daily positive affirmations. Finally, crystals for specific ailments, disorders, disease, and crystal prescriptions will be explained in detail.

We have all experienced stress in a multitude of ways and on different levels including the physical, mental, and emotional. Learning the benefits of crystal healing can help balance our lives in order to feel less stressed and more energized. Some of the information in this book will allow you to open your mind, body, and spirit to the healing properties of crystals to help alleviate common stressors you may be experiencing. You will also realize how crystals initiate the power to self-heal.

This book is intended to provide you with basic information in order to utilize the functional relevance of powerful earth element crystals in your daily life. You may begin to notice small shifts at first. As you become more familiar with the practical applications of crystal use, you may experience significant changes for the better.

There are plenty of books about crystals and their healing powers on the market. Thank you so much for choosing this one! Every effort was made to ensure it is full of as much useful information as possible.

CHAPTER 1
Properties And Powers Of Crystals

What Are Crystals, Gems, Minerals, and Rocks?

Crystals are natural elements that come from the Earth. A true crystal has an organized grouping of unit cells that form a unique lattice pattern called a crystal system. There are six lattice patterns that appear within healing crystals. There is also a category of stones known as amorphous crystals, even though they are not truly crystals as they do not have an interior crystalline structure. Some of these include amber, obsidian, and opal. They each have their own unique properties.

Some use the words crystal, gem, mineral, and rock interchangeably, especially in the metaphysical aspect pertaining to crystals. Some materials that are not crystals such as amber, which is petrified tree sap, are also referred to as crystals or stones. There are technical differences among each of these. Crystals are made of minerals that are made of elements. Crystals are sometimes called gems. Crystals can be found in rocks.

Element
The chemical components of the earth are considered elements. Silver, gold, and iron are examples of elements that on their own make up crystals.

Crystal
A crystal is a mineral that has a crystalline interior structure. Agate, which is a hexagonal crystal, is also a mineral and a rock.

Gem
A gem is a cut and polished crystal, mineral, or rock. A cut diamond, which is a mineral, a crystal, and a rock, is also a gem or gemstone. Amber and pearls are organic substances that are considered gemstones but are not crystals, minerals, or rocks. Some gems come from organic matter rather than minerals. Pearls, amber, and coral are in this category. Even though they are not technically crystals, they are still used in crystal healing.

Mineral
A substance that occurs naturally with a highly ordered structure that may or may not be crystalline and with a specific chemical composition. Opal is a mineral that does not have a crystalline structure. It is a gemstone and a rock but not a true crystal.

Rock
A rock is a combination of minerals. Marble, which is made up of multiple minerals, is a metamorphic rock. It is a rock that has been subjected to heat and pressure over time.

Patterns of Crystals

Crystals are made up of three-dimensional patterns consisting of atoms, ions, or molecules.

The six crystal lattice patterns include the following:

Hexagonal - Hexagonal crystals have an interior structure that resembles a 3-D hexagon. Hexagonal crystals help with manifestation.

Isometric - Isometric crystals have an interior cubic structure. These crystals can amplify energies and improve situations.

Monoclinic - Monoclinic crystals have a 3-D parallelogram structure. They are protective crystals.

Orthorhombic - Orthorhombic crystals have a diamond-shaped crystalline pattern. They remove blockages, cleanse, and clear.

Tetragonal - Tetragonal crystals have a rectangular interior structure. These crystals are attractors. They make things more attractive and they help you attract things to you.

Triclinic - Triclinic crystals have an interior structure with three inclined axes. These crystals ward off unwanted energies or help retain energies you would like to keep.

Choosing Your Crystals

Crystals are readily available at metaphysical type stores or online. There are also many crystals, minerals, and gem shows that travel all over. It may cost to get into the show, but most vendors there are very knowledgeable. Crystals are fairly inexpensive, so stocking up on the main healing ones as well as extras you may be drawn to are pretty attainable. Be sure to store any you purchase in a soft cloth bag and if keeping all together, include clear quartz to keep them clear. When using a crystal, you can hold it, place it around you, or tape it to a specific area or organ needing healing, or even wear it in a metal spiral around your neck. Crystals usually activate well directly on your skin. Most work through clothes however and can still be beneficial this way. Keeping crystals in your pocket can also help. This can make it easy to access too, especially for a stress relieving stone.

You will inevitably have crystals choose you. However, you will be drawn to one or more just for their shape, color, size, purpose, or properties. Once you have a crystal collection of your own, you will then have stones to choose from for a specific purpose. Even then, choosing the right one for the job can seem daunting. There are a few tips you can follow to be certain you are finding the best match.

You can ask yourself "Which crystal do I need?" and listen for the answer. Asking this removes any preconceived notions. What you may think you need to be healed isn't actually what needs healing. Your subconscious can guide you in the right direction so listening to that is one of the most efficient ways in selecting the appropriate crystal.

Read through a multitude of listings of crystal properties and subsequent conditions, such as the ones in this book or online. There are many helpful websites to sort through to help pick a particular crystal. Metaphysical stores can also help. Salespeople at them are usually there because they have unique knowledge about the usages of crystals, or they have hands-on experience in using them.

You can choose a crystal based on color and crystal system or how the crystal's shape is made up. Use your best knowledge to guide you to a crystal that's right for that moment.

Muscle testing, a form of Applied Kinesiology, AK, can also be used to help choose a crystal. Kinesiology is a study of how muscles move, voluntarily or involuntarily. It is defined as the use of muscle testing to pinpoint imbalances in the body's physical, chemical, and emotional energy. It allows a person or practitioner to evaluate energy changes and decide the exact healing needs of the body on all levels. It is commonly used in sports medicine and chiropractic practices. It can also apply to choosing and using crystals. There are simple techniques anyone can use to test the effects of the subconscious mind on the muscles.

Place a crystal anywhere on you. With your giving or dominant hand, extend your pointer finger and press down on it with your middle finger of the same hand, resisting a bit with your pointer finger. If your pointer finger holds strong, you do not need that crystal at that time. If you cannot hold strong and the hold is weak, that is the crystal to work with. You can also muscle test while standing. Raise your right arm and hand so it is parallel to the floor. Hold a crystal in your receiving or non-dominant hand. Ask a partner or other person to push down gently on your right hand with just their right or left hand. Do this before, during, and after holding the crystal in your left hand. Before holding the crystal, ask if it is needed right now. If when the other person pushes on your right hand, there is strong resistance, that is a "yes" and a good crystal to use. If the hold is weak and your arm easily goes down, that is a "no" and not a good crystal to use.

Applied Kinesiology could be used to figure out if a crystal needs clearing or not. If it contains a lot of negative energy, it will test as a "yes" when asked if it needs cleansing. You could also use Applied Kinesiology when starting a crystal collection, to muscle test "yes" or "no" if a crystal is good for you in general or not.

Use your intuition and your gut feeling when choosing a crystal too. Trust in your subconscious mind giving you clues. Trust yourself that you will use the crystal you choose in the right way that will benefit your higher self. When you do this and trust yourself, everyone benefits in the long run. This is part of the healing process and being aware we are all part of a bigger picture together.

The following catalog of crystals is only an abbreviated list of types of earth stones that can aid common ailments and disorders, as well as help to regulate balance and wellbeing. There are so many more crystals available to you than on the following pages. However, the ones listed are the core healers as well as most common to find and own. Crystals are useful to keep us balanced on a daily basis, but they can also be very beneficial in healing. The list describes the properties of each crystal, its characteristics, and how you can benefit from them. As you read through the list and each description, see which ones stand out to you. As healing usually occurs on more than one level simultaneously, you may be attracted to more than one crystal at a time.

Tips for Crystal Choosing

Ground yourself before you go or enter a crystal shop or show. Many crystals in one spot can be disorienting. If you feel dizzy or lightheaded while in a shop or at a crystal show, imagine strong roots growing from your feet into the ground. Pick up any black stone until you feel stabilized.

Asking questions at a gem show or in a metaphysical shop can help guide you in the right direction for choosing crystals, especially in the beginning of starting a collection. Shop owners, workers, and vendors can be a valuable resource. They are usually in the business because they have hands-on experience in using crystals and are knowledgeable about their healing qualities and properties. They can be a lifelong source of information and are usually more than willing to answer any questions relating to crystals and gems.

Go where you are drawn to and pay attention. If there is a particular location in a shop or gem show you are drawn to, go to it. Then see which crystal draws you to it. This helps initiate your intuitive process and the choosing of crystals.

Touch and handle the crystals. Get a feel for what their energies feel like. See how they actually make you feel when handling them.

You can quickly intent them to be clear and cleansed, free of anyone else's energy, so you can get their actual vibration. If anyone in a shop or at a gem show does not let you feel or hold a stone, do not buy from them and go elsewhere.

Try to do research before going to a crystal shop or gem show. Check a seller's reputation if you can. Read reviews if they are available. Check for articles online or elsewhere.

Don't always buy the first thing you see. It is easy to be overwhelmed when you go to a store or show that has an overabundance of pretty, shiny, sparkly stones. Take your time and learn about the crystals and products available. You can even get a feel for different prices of the same stones by comparing stores or websites. Find the best price for the crystals that appeal to you most.

If you do not recognize a crystal by its name, ask if it is trademarked. If it is, ask for the generic version. You can look it up online or on your phone. You can also use an app to see if it is a trademarked crystal or a less expensive generic version. You can search under "Healing Crystals."

Crystal Catalog

Amazonite
Amazonite's healing powers help with emotional issues, physical ailments, in energy healing, and chakra balancing. Its light green, blue-green or aquamarine color works with the heart and throat chakras. In this way, it is a loving communication crystal. It is often called the Stone of Truth and Stone of Courage, allowing those who use it to bravely speak and live their authentic self. Amazonite is thought to be a calming, balancing stone. Its appearance can be either natural and tumbled or smooth and polished. Amazonite helps communicate your true thoughts and feelings without too much emotion. When you keep Amazonite near or wear it as jewelry, it can enable you to see things from a different perspective, thus allowing one to be objective. This crystal can help balance one's own inner turmoil. Amazonite also helps with forgiveness,

peace and understanding, integrity, prosperity, protection, and loving one's self and others unconditionally.

Amber
Amber is not technically a crystal but has such healing properties that it is used extensively in the naturopath and metaphysical world. It has an affiliation with both the sun and the earth with its golden color. It is also connected to insects and nature that may become eternally suspended in its hardened sap. Amber is best known to relieve inflammation and the pain associated with it. It can appear natural or cut and is characteristically golden, brown, honey colored. Amber is good for the solar plexus chakra. It helps with creating positive energy, self-esteem, increasing life force, and averting others' energy.

Amethyst
Amethyst is a form of quartz most commonly purple. It has strong healing powers and is especially useful in providing pain relief. You can place an amethyst crystal directly on a part of your body in pain and it will gently draw it out while releasing any stuck energy. In this way, it is very effective in relieving tension headaches and migraines by placing directly on your forehead or sinuses. Amethyst crystals help with intuition and insight, connecting to higher self and the Divine, insomnia, stress, anxiety, safe travel, nightmares, and addiction. It is associated with the third eye and crown chakras. Its shape can appear natural, in points, clusters, geodes, tumbled and polished, or cut. Amethyst is a wonderfully versatile stone.

Ametrine
Ametrine is a beautiful crystal with clear purple and yellow colorings. It has the ability to combine and amplify the properties of both amethyst and citrine crystals as they naturally form in this one crystal. It is highly effective at increasing prosperity, abundance, psychic communication, aura cleansing, transmuting negativity, positive energy flow, balancing opposite energy characteristics, and promoting spiritual dreaming, and balancing of spirit with human energies. Ametrine is associated with the solar plexus chakra as well as the third eye and crown chakra. It appears naturally, in points, clusters, tumbled and polished, or cut. You can place ametrine on the solar plexus region, third eye chakra, near

the crown of your head, or head of your bed when working with it. Wearing an ametrine necklace will help motivate and balance the flow of the energy from the solar plexus through the crown chakras.

Apache Tears
The legend of Apache Tears is a sacred one. Anyone with this healing stone should be aware of its history. In the 1870s an Apache tribe hid on a ridge in Arizona from US Cavalry they supposedly stole cattle and supplies from. Their land had been under siege for a long time and they were being attacked. 50 of 75 Apache died under a quick surprise attack on the cliff. The other 25 Apache warriors chose to jump off rather than be killed by the white man. Apache women and family of those who died gathered below and cried for a moon. It is said their tears fell onto white sand, turning to black obsidian stones that held their tears. Anyone with an Apache Tear stone does not need to cry for the Apache Women have done it for them and the grief is no more. Apache Tears are actually obsidian stones from volcanic glass, usually round or oval in shape, varying in color from dark gray to deep black. These stones are extremely effective in helping to overcome grief, sadness, or dark emotions. They are beneficial to the root chakra, thus a balancing stone. It is believed if you wear or carry Apache Tear stones when dealing with the death of a loved one, you can use them as worry stones to stop grief from becoming overwhelming.

Apatite
Apatite is a beautiful blue-green stone associated with deep spiritual wisdom and truth. It is a soft crystal that can be brittle. It should be stored separately and carefully away from other crystals. Apatite is an amplifying crystal that can aid in focusing on goals, eliminating negativity, raising energetic vibrations, connecting to the Divine, enhancing intuition, and increasing truth and motivation. It also works with decreasing social anxiety and self-consciousness. The root, solar plexus, heart, throat, third eye, and crown chakras are the chakras associated with apatite. It appears in a natural state, as points, tumbled and polished, or cut.

Aquamarine
Aquamarine is a manifestation stone with a brilliant yet calming blue-green color. It can appear natural or pointed, tumbled and polished, or cut. The chakras related to it are the heart, throat, and

third eye. This crystal can help with aligning and balancing all of the chakras, soothing anxiety, decreasing phobias, assisting with manifestation, courage, protection, self-expression, and spiritual truth.

Aventurine

Aventurine is created by a mixture of quartz and other minerals which lend to its coloring. They can be blue, green, red, orange, yellow or white, but green is the most common color. Since green is associated with healing in general and the heart chakra, green Aventurine is said to be the ultimate healing stone while also promoting prosperity. It can enable you to live by the desires of your own heart. It can also help get rid of illness or disease tied to old emotions. This allows anyone with the stone to break free from old habits and get to the underlying reason for the disease. It can help with conditions of the heart and blood pressure, as well as relieve manic type stress or overproduction of adrenaline due to chronic tension. Its appearance can be natural, pointed, tumbled and polished, or cut. Other chakras associated with the other colors of Aventurine are red for root, orange for sacral, yellow for solar plexus, blue for throat and third eye, white for crown.

Bloodstone

Bloodstone gets its name from the opaque green appearance with lines of blood red jasper Bloodstone, also known as Heliotrope, is a master healer for the body as it relieves chronic conditions such as fatigue and with revitalizing effects on a person's immune system. It can help with auto-immune diseases such as thyroiditis and rheumatoid arthritis. Bloodstone is also a strong detoxifier. It cleanses the blood and lymph to remove waste and toxins from blood-rich organs and body tissues. It can be placed in the bath to increase blood flow and circulation. Bloodstone aligns with the heart, root, and lower chakras. It can have a raw cut appearance or tumbled and polished.

Blue Lace Agate

Blue lace agate is a nurturing crystal with a gentle, cooling energy. It is a powerful throat cleanser and healer, thus benefits the throat chakra and thyroid and parathyroid glands. It aids in opening lines of communication and activating that which has previously been held back. It is a gentle stone that allows built up energy to rise to the surface slowly to finally be released and let go. It stabilizes heat from a fever, inflammation, and infection, while its calming energy promotes peace of mind. Agate is a very holistic healer that works on balancing all levels, including physical, emotional, mental, and spiritual. It helps to relieve tension in the neck and shoulders and chest and lung congestion which can be associated with grief. Agate is good for relieving arthritis, asthma, bones and circulation issues. It appears natural, tumbled and polished, or cut.

Bronzite
Bronzite is a brown, usually speckled and tumbled stone associated with all the chakras. It is a protective, activating, grounding crystal. It can help with figuring out what it is you want to achieve in your life, promotes certainty and control, calmness, enhances creativity and forward thinking. It allows you to think objectively and see the bigger picture. Bronzite can help alleviate anxiety associated with starting something new or being in a new situation such as a social one. It can dispel negative energy, ease stress, warm the extremities, aid in digestion, supports kidney function, balance the body's pH levels, and enhances the assimilation of iron, making it a good stone for anemia.

Calcite
Calcite comes in a rainbow of colors, each with specific properties associated with the chakras with which they align. It is an excellent manifestation stone as it naturally helps in achieving desires. It is also an amplifying crystal. It helps with cleansing, grounding, inner peace, speaking your truth, integrity, abundance, unconditional love, self-esteem, intuition, personal will, communicating with a higher power, and spiritual growth. The different colors aid in corresponding chakras are as follows: red, black or gray with the root chakra; orange or peach, sacral; green or pink, heart; purple, third eye; honey or yellow, solar plexus; blue, throat; white, crown. Create a relaxing and peaceful environment by placing different colored calcite stones around a room such as bedroom, bathroom, or living room. Calcites appear naturally, tumbled and polished, or cut.

Carnelian
Carnelian is associated with boldness, courage, life, and vitality. It

is a very energetic crystal. You would not want to keep it near your bedside table or wherever you rest. Do keep it on your desk or workspace to increase energy throughout the day. Its brownish red to red-orange coloring is associated with the root and sacral chakras. These chakras have to do with creativity, physical energy, safety in ourselves and with others, fertility/sexuality, and happiness. It can be used to improve strength, sense of self, and humility. It can help you set proper boundaries. Carnelian has been used to help vocalists as well as public speakers increase courage and bring strength to the voice. Its shape can be natural, tumbled and polished, or cut.

Chalcedony
Chalcedony is a form of quartz that gets its color from mineral occlusions. Agates are a form of chalcedony, as is carnelian. However, when discussing healing crystals, chalcedony typically refers to a creamy blue variety of the stone. Known as the Speaker's Stone, it helps you speak your truth with fact. Chalcedony also helps with manifestation, creativity, promoting peace, lessening self-doubt, and balancing emotions. It is associated with the throat chakra and communication. It is an amplifying crystal. Place chalcedony close to your lips, tongue, or mouth before public speaking to help you speak truthfully and well. Chalcedony appears naturally, as geodes, tumbled and polished, or cut. They are very useful in necklaces and earrings, wearing directly on the throat chakra, or in a chest pocket close to it.

Citrine
Citrine is a powerful golden-yellow and clear crystal associated with the solar plexus chakra. It appears naturally, in clusters, tumbled and polished, or cut. If placed in the back left corner of your home or business, it is thought to bring prosperity. It also helps with self-esteem, creativity, thinking clearly, manifestations, asserting personal will, and bringing forth new beginnings. It dispels negativity while increasing positive feelings. It is a good stone for depression, self-doubt, anger, and mood swings. It can bring you happiness, strength, and success.

Clear Quartz
Clear quartz is considered by many to be the most versatile and powerful of the master healing stones. It works through any and all

conditions. If you are beginning a crystal collection, clear quartz is a wonderful first choice. It contains the full spectrum of visible light and links the physical body with emotions, the mind, and spirit. Clear quartz is a terrific conductor and increaser of energy. It can strengthen any crystal's power just by being near it. It also clears all other crystals while being self-cleansing. It helps with balance, protection, cleansing, purification, healing on all levels, amplifying energy and thought, connecting to higher consciousness and the Divine, and improving concentration. It is an excellent overall healing and clearing stone and for using in crystal grids. This crystal uniquely attunes itself to your individual needs and adjusts its healing energy accordingly. It is mostly associated with the crown chakra for its effectiveness in meditation and connecting to your higher self, but it can benefit all chakras equally. It is a clear to milky white crystal appearing naturally, polished, cut, in points, geodes, or clusters.

Danburite
Danburite comes in multiple colors that affect different chakras. However, all colors are high vibration stones associated with spiritual enlightenment and connection to a higher power. It is also a cleansing and clearing stone that can help to heal deep emotional pain and wounds. Danburite appears naturally or tumbled and polished as clear, gray, or green. Green danburite is associated with the heart chakra, clear and gray with the crown chakra. It is a crystal that helps with intuition, deep emotional healing, compassion and unconditional love, connecting the upper chakras heart through crown, easing transitions, calming, stress relief, purifying the aura, and cleansing. Danburite is an excellent meditation stone when you wish to connect with your higher power. Hold it in either hand as you meditate. You can place danburite on the heart or crown chakra directly, in a pocket during stressful times, around the home to promote healing energy throughout.

Emerald
Emerald is actually a form of a mineral called beryl. Other beryls include aquamarine and morganite. Emerald is often cut and polished and made into jewelry as it is well-known. With its characteristic green color, emerald is a classic heart chakra stone that promotes love and compassion. It helps with prosperity,

unconditional love, compassion, romance, kindness, forgiveness, manifestation, increasing spiritual awareness, serenity, experiencing Divine love, protection, and healing trauma. Emerald can be placed directly on the heart chakra, worn as jewelry or specifically as a ring on the commitment finger. They are often given as a promise or engagement stone. Emerald is a hard stone but has a lot of inclusions so can break easily.

Epidote

Epidote is a protective stone primarily associated with the heart chakra and love. It can help improve interpersonal relationships, creating a balance between partners, and enhancing love and personal growth. It also amplifies the energy of other stones. Epidote helps with prosperity, love, connection with nature, optimism, grounding, clearing energetic blockages, strengthening, and stimulating healing. Its green color connects it to the heart chakra and issues relating to love. You can place Epidote directly on the heart chakra, hold in your hand after meditation for grounding, and next to any other stone you wish to increase the effectiveness of. If you live in the city or haven't been outdoors in a while, you can meditate with Epidote to connect to the natural world.

Fluorite

Fluorite is a soft mineral crystal that can chip easily. It should be used and stored very carefully. Fluorite can range in coloration from light green to deep purple all in one stone. For this reason, it is often called rainbow fluorite. Fluorite helps with calming and balancing energies and emotions. It is a good connector of body, mind, and spirit as well as with assisting in communication with higher planes and the Divine, intuition, enhancing creativity, peace, and wellbeing. It can be a gentle healer and is often used by natural practitioners to encourage slow but steady self-healing. It is associated with the heart, throat, third eye, and crown chakras.

Fuschite

Fuschite is a sparkling green silicate mineral embedded with mica. It can also often have ruby embedded in it. It is a protective stone and a classic healer's stone that can help with physical, energetic, and emotional healing. Fuschite is a soft stone that must be stored carefully and away from other crystals because of this. It is associated with the heart chakra. It helps with healing on all levels — physical, emotional, mental, and spiritual, rejuvenation, balance, prosperity, love, intensifying energy with other crystals. It can be placed on the heart chakra, if embedded with ruby, it can be placed on the root chakra and heart chakra, or worn as a necklace or bracelet.

Garnet
Garnets are commonly a red stone called pyrope everyone is familiar with. They can also be yellow to orange and brown and called spessartine garnet, and green garnets are called tsavorite garnets. Garnets are a protection, manifestation, and amplifier of energy crystal. They also boost energy, help with transitions, overcoming trauma, and getting rid of limiting ideas and beliefs. They are good for career success and moving forward, getting out of the past. If you are going through a lot of changes or a transition, wear or carry garnet to help ease the shift. In this way, garnet can be a very overall useful crystal while healing. Wearing garnets in rings or bracelets is very popular and beneficial. Garnet appears naturally, in points, clusters, tumbled and polished, or cut.

Hematite
Hematite is a shiny, black pearlescent stone used for absorbing negative energy. It is a protective, grounding, balancing, detoxifying crystal. It is strongly associated with the root chakra but can also benefit the solar plexus chakra. A lot of jewelry is made of hematite. Wearing it can help us feel grounded or connected to the earth so it can be good in stressful situations. It helps the mind focus, stimulates concentration, memory, and original thought. It can also help us release old thoughts or feelings without realizing it for our greater good. Hematite is the mineral form of iron oxide thus aids in all blood disorders, restoring and regulating blood supply. It can be natural, polished, cut, or in rings. Hematite absorbs a lot of negative energy so is often over-worked. It can break easily because of this.

Howlite
Howlite is a white to light grey colored stone with dark grey to black lines in it. It is a crown chakra stone that helps in connecting to higher truth, linking users of the stone to the Divine. It also aids in calming anxiety, reducing stress, and easing intense negative

emotions such as anger and rage. It appears natural, tumbled or polished, carved, and cut. Howlite is a soft stone easily carved into jewelry, benefiting the crown chakra by wearing earrings or a necklace close to it. The jewelry can have a calming effect during high stress or tense situations.

Jade
Jade has been used since ancient times, often carved into jewelry or other statues and artifacts. Most people recognize green jade but it may also be white or even orange. It appears naturally you can hang, tumbled or polished, and carved. Since jade has been of value and is extremely popular in many cultures for so many centuries, there are a lot of imitations. True jade should have irregularities under close inspection and should be looked for. Jade helps with protection, easing guilt, disrupting negative thought patterns, safe travel, reducing excessive wanting of power, strengthening life force energies, increasing trust, and promoting love of all kind. Jade can be worn as jewelry or in a pocket on any of the corresponding chakras. Chakras Jade is associated with are red, black, or gray jade with the root chakra; orange, sacral; yellow, solar plexus; green, heart; blue, throat; purple, third eye; white, crown chakra.

Jasper
Jasper is a cosmically colorful stone. There are multiple opaque colors and varieties of Jasper, which is actually a combination of quartz or chalcedony and other minerals. Different varieties have varying properties. In general, however, Jasper is a manifestation stone that absorbs excess energies to help with energetic balance. It can appear naturally, tumbled and polished, carved, or cut. Jasper is an absorbing crystal rock. It is associated with the following chakras according to corresponding colors: Red or black, root; orange, sacral; yellow or brown, solar plexus; green, heart; blue, throat or third eye. It helps with manifestation, grounding, stability, balancing excess energies associated with addiction, and obsessive-compulsive behavior. You can hold jasper after meditation for grounding. It can be worn on any of the chakras, as jewelry, or in a pocket.

Kyanite

While blue is the most common color of kyanite, it also comes in yellow, green, black, and orange. It is a brittle stone that is often blade shaped which makes it a good worry stone for rubbing your thumb across. Kyanite never needs cleansing because it does not hold on to energy. It just facilitates energy's movement. This is also why neither absorption nor amplification is noted for this crystal. Kyanite helps with creating pathways from one thing to another, clearing blockages, getting you out of rut, initiating communication, loyalty and fairness, memory recall, and grounding. It appears as natural, in blades, tumbled and polished, carved, and cut. Chakras associated with corresponding colors of kyanite are black or gray, root chakra; orange, sacral; yellow, solar plexus; green, heart; blue, throat or third eye; white, crown chakra. You can place this crystal on any of the corresponding chakras, in a pocket, or in your hand as a worry stone. You can also use kyanite between other crystals in a grid to facilitate energy flow from one crystal to the next.

Labradorite
Labradorite is a magical crystal that can enhance intuition, psychic, and mystical abilities by raising consciousness and dissolving illusions. It will clear your aura and close it for protection. It is a very spiritual healing stone, stress reliever, and can help lower blood pressure. It harmonizes all of the subtle outside bodies with the physical body. Labradorite is an opalescent stone with a gleaming blue or gray base. When it is not cut or polished, it looks like a regular rough rock. It assuredly aligns with the crown chakra as well as throat and third eye.

Lapis Lazuli
Lapis lazuli isn't technically a crystal, because it doesn't have a crystalline structure. Rather, it is a metamorphic rock. However, it has been recognized for centuries as a semiprecious stone having magical powers. The sarcophagus of King Tutankhamen is decorated with lapis lazuli, as are many other ancient artifacts. Lapis lazuli helps with communication of all types, particularly written, learning, encouraging honesty and speaking one's truth, harmony, and improving performance. It is a performer's stone. Wear it for auditions or public speaking engagements to help provide a perfect performance.

Larimar
Larimar is a calming, tranquil stone that forms in lava. It is also known as the Atlantis Stone or the Dolphin Stone found only in the Dominican Republic. It is the blue version of the stone pectolite and can be white, light to deep blue, green blue and have a milky or translucent appearance to it, reminiscent of the Caribbean waters it is found in. It is thought to be a remnant from Atlantis and to have the ability to help in communicating with dolphins. It appears natural, in blades, tumbled or polished, and carved. It is an absorbing stone that works well with clear quartz and selenite. Larimar helps with many healings including relaxation, calming and soothing, promoting peace and serenity, clarifying dream meanings, assisting in resolving trauma, and giving voice to wisdom. It is associated with the throat and third eye chakra. You can place it on the throat chakra, next to your bed, or taped under the head of your bed to assist in its usages. Wear larimar as a necklace when it is important to speak your truth calmly and wisely.

Lodestone
Lodestone, also called magnetite, is a black magnetic stone made from iron oxide and is very amplifying. You can find it with small pieces of iron stuck to it from magnetism. If you do find it this way, be sure to store it away from other crystals so you can retain the small pieces of iron with it. Lodestone helps with grounding, protection, and attracting what you create. You can place it near the root chakra, in a bracelet. It is a very strong stone and should probably be stored in a protective container even when being used. It is associated with the root chakra. It can be found naturally, natural with iron stuck to it, or tumbled and polished.

Malachite
Malachite is a beautiful deep green color with bands of lighter and darker green through it. It is a stone of the heart, nature, prosperity, and healing. It absorbs energy and is associated with the heart chakra. Malachite helps with absorbing negative energy, guarding against energetic and physical pollution, protecting against accidents, and relieving fears associated with travel. Malachite is believed to offer protection during air travel. Carry a small piece in a carry-on handbag when you fly. You can place malachite on or near the heart chakra, as a necklace or bracelet.

Moonstone
Moonstone is a variety of feldspar characterized by its milky white color with an opalescent sheen. It is a good stone for new beginnings as well as connecting to higher realms, Divinity, and intuition. It provides protection while traveling by water or by night. It aligns with the third eye and crown chakra. Moonstone can provide calmness by soothing emotional instability and stress. It appears naturally or tumbled and polished or cut. It is associated with the third eye and crown chakras.

Obsidian
Obsidian is a type of volcanic glass but has many healing qualities. It is usually shiny black but can also have specks of white and be known also as snowflake obsidian. Obsidian is a root chakra stone that is very grounding and protective. It helps to protect against negativity and is good for clearing your aura. It is also helpful in releasing anger and resentment. If you are feeling foggy or energetically stuck, hold a piece of obsidian in your receiving, dominant hand, while breathing evenly and deeply.

Onyx
Onyx is a variety of chalcedony with parallel bands in the stone. It is a black, protective, and grounding stone that can also aid in manifestation and it can help balance excessive sexual desire. Onyx absorbs energy and is associated with the root chakra. You can place it on or near the root chakra or in a pair of a pants pocket. Onyx helps with grounding, improving harmony in intimate relationships, improving self-control, calming worry and tension, and soothing nightmares. To use onyx efficiently, put it on your bedside table or taped to a headboard to help balance intimate relationships.

Opal
Opals are highly valued as a gemstone and a healing stone. They have a beautiful, soft rainbow, luminescent quality to them. However, because opals do not have a crystalline structure, they are technically not regarded as crystals. Opals are soft with a high water content, which makes them particularly delicate. They can be colorless, white, and yellow, violet, red, pink, orange, green,

blue, and black. Root chakra is related to red or black opals, sacral relates to orange, solar plexus on yellow, the heart chakra on green or pink, throat on blue, violet the third eye, the crown and higher chakras on colorless or white. You should never clean an opal in water or with chemicals, including opal jewelry pieces. They are natural, tumbled and polished, or cut. They have amplifying energy qualities so they will help increase the power of other crystals. They help with creativity, dreams, connection to the Divine and higher self, facilitating the flow of transformation, assisting in moving easily through obstacles, improving memory and inspiration. You can place opals near the head of your bed for meditation and dreaming, on or near any chakra, and as a jewelry of any type. It is considered good luck to receive an opal piece of jewelry from someone else. Opal is very popular in jewelry. It is important to store opals carefully, away from other crystals to prevent damage as they are so soft.

Peridot
Peridot has a beautiful green color that makes it very popular and highly valued as a gemstone. It is also known as olivine or chrysolite. It is a stone of unconditional love, compassion, forgiveness, and other heart associated experiences and emotions. It is also a cleansing and clearing stone. Peridot appears naturally, tumbled or polished, and cut. It is an amplifying crystal associated with the heart chakra. It helps with promoting positivity, forgiveness, all types of love, prosperity, luck, healing emotional trauma, lessening ego, aura cleansing, and balancing all the chakras. You can carry or wear peridot when you feel like you need a little extra luck or feelings of love. It is a very popular gemstone for jewelry pieces. Wear it on or near your heart chakra as a necklace, or as a bracelet or ring on your commitment finger. Periodot works well with clear quartz, rose quartz, and smoky quartz.

Rhodochrosite
Rhodochrosite is a vibrant, banded pink stone. The lighter pink varieties can be often confused with rose quartz. Because of the color similarities, it does have some of the similar metaphysical properties of rose quartz. In general, however, you can tell it is rhodochrosite instead of rose quartz by its intense, deep pink color and the white bands running through it. It does appear in its

natural state, tumbled and polished, or cut. The deep pink varieties can be associated with the root chakra. The lighter pink crystals are associated with the heart chakra. Rhodochrosite helps with unconditional love, compassion, kindness, calming, grounding, self-compassion, forgiveness, and aura cleansing. If you are struggling with self-compassion or self-love issues, hold rhodochrosite in your receiving, non-dominant hand as you state firmly, "I love myself unconditionally." You can also place it on or near your root or heart chakra, wear as a necklace or bracelet, or as a ring on your commitment finger. It works well with rose quartz and clear quartz and it is an amplifying crystal.

Rose Quartz
The crystal of unconditional love, compassion, and kindness. It exudes forgiveness, self-love and healing, and overall feelings of joy. It helps in feeling connected to others with peace and calmness. Although green is usually associated with the heart chakra, rose quartz is definitely a heart chakra stone. It is a wonderful stone for self-forgiveness or self-healing, break up, betrayal, and handling emotions with losing a family or a loved one. It appears naturally as a pale, clear pink stone tumbled and polished, cut, in points, or clusters.

Ruby
Ruby is a vibrant red, precious gemstone. Rubies and sapphires are forms of corundum, a valued mineral. Along with finding ruby crystals by themselves, you can also find them embedded in fuchsite or zoisite. Rubies found this way can be more affordable yet still contain all the properties of a single ruby. It is a crystal associated with the root and heart chakras. Ruby helps with all types of love, opening the heart, expressing love, compassion, trust, courage, forgiveness, grounding, clearing blocked energies and emotions, and connecting to spiritual and Divine love. If you feel stuck in any emotion, wear ruby jewelry or carry a gem with you or in a pocket to help you break free of the emotion. It can be worn as any jewelry such as necklace, bracelet, or ring on your commitment finger. Place it on or near your root or heart chakra for effectiveness as well. It is an amplifying stone that works with sapphire and rose quartz. Ruby can appear naturally, tumbled and polished, or cut.

Sapphire

Similarly to rubies, sapphire is a form of the valued mineral corundum. Most people think of sapphires being only blue, but this gemstone also comes in a variety of colors including orange, yellow, and pink. The popular deep blue sapphire is associated with the third eye or throat chakra; orange with sacral; yellow with solar plexus; and pink with the third eye chakra. It is a stone for protection and manifestation. Sapphire helps with self-expression, communication, speaking personal truth, loyalty, surrendering of personal will to Divine will, and sleep issues. It works well with ruby. Sapphire is particularly powerful when used with some type of vocal meditations such as mantra meditations. It can be placed on or near the appropriate chakra, especially the throat chakra, as a necklace or earrings, or near the head of your bed for insomnia.

Selenite
A variety of gypsum, selenite is a very soft crystal. Because of this, it is easy to carve and you will often find it carved into interesting shapes, towers, and wands. It is primarily a protective stone and is a soft, pearly white. It is also a crystal that does not absorb or store energy so it does not need cleansing. It serves as a cleansing stone for other crystals. It is also an amplifying stone associated with the third eye and crown chakra. It appears naturally, carved, cut or tumbled, and polished. Selenite helps with protecting against negativity, cleansing negative energy, forgiveness, cleansing other crystals, cleansing the aura, and connection with intuition and the Divine. You can place it on or near the third eye or crown chakra. It works well with all other crystals. Due to selenite's softness, it can get damaged easily and should be stored separately from other crystals. Never expose it to water or salt.

Sodalite
Sodalite is a natural amplifier that balances energies if you have too much of one and not enough of another. It can be deep blue to light blue, with white and black. It eliminates confusion and unites logic with intuition, enabling you to find your inner truth. It is helpful in overcoming repeated patterns, phobias, and panic attacks. It can help in group situations by encouraging trust and everyone to speak their true selves. Sodalite resonates with the throat and third eye chakras. It can also be useful in absorbing electromagnetic smog, radiation damage, and emanations from electronics. It can

help to keep sodalite at your workplace to help dispel. It appears naturally, tumbled and polished, carved, or cut.

Tanzanite

Tanzanite can help release things that no longer serve you. It can also help clear energetic blockages and get rid of unwanted energy. This gem is named after where it was discovered, Tanzania. It is a violet-blue stone, thus associated with the throat, third eye, and even crown chakra. It is an amplifying crystal that helps with clearing away unwanted energy and things that don't serve you, aiding in self-discovery and discovery of your true spiritual nature, promoting connection to higher self and to the Divine, and integrating third eye and crown chakras. It appears natural, tumbled and polished, carved, or cut. Place it on or near the throat, third eye, or crown chakra, wear as earrings, or a necklace. Tanzanite can help you discover and clarify your own spiritual beliefs. To help with this, hold it in your receiving, non-dominant hand during meditation or a prayer or affirmation. It works well with clear quartz and celestite.

Tiger's Eye

Tiger's Eye is a manifestation stone and can help issues with self-esteem or self-worth. It has a rich layering of yellow and brown that shimmers in the light. Tiger's eye can also be blue or red. It is a protective stone that promotes balance and connection to the earth. It relates to the root, solar plexus, and throat chakras. It helps with self-expression, self-love, self-criticism, and manifesting goals. It increases willpower, emotional stability, and psychic abilities. Place on the third eye during meditation to connect to higher realms and Divinity. Tiger's eye appears natural, tumbled and polished, carved, or cut. It is very popular in wearing jewelry such as earrings, bracelets, and necklaces.

Topaz

Topaz is an exceptionally clear gemstone that can help you cleanse energies and release things that no longer serve you. It can also help to align and balance energies. Golden topaz is the most commonly known form of the crystal, but other colors can occur as well including blue, colorless, green, peach, pink, red, and yellow. Red topaz relates to the root chakra, peach on sacral, green on heart, yellow or gold on solar plexus, pink on third eye, blue on throat, and clear or colorless on crown chakra. Topaz appears naturally, in clusters, tumbled and polished, carved, or cut. It is an amplifying crystal that works well with tanzanite and celestite. It helps with self-expression, self-worth, self-esteem, self-definition, self-love, self-criticism, self-concept, manifesting creative vision, and manifesting goals. You can place topaz on or near the appropriate chakra you are working with, as any type of jewelry, around the perimeter, or in the corners of any room that you want cleared of negative energy. Hold or wear topaz when you state your affirmations or as you work on any creative projects.

Tourmaline (Including Black)
Tourmaline is a powerful mental healer. It helps to balance both right and left hemispheres of the brain so it can be very beneficial for those dealing with dyslexia, paranoia, hand-eye coordination, and speech. It is a protection stone and is used to bring about a feeling of overall wellbeing. Tourmaline is excellent in releasing stagnant energy to remove blockages. Natural tourmaline wands can be held over chakras to address what needs to be cleared for healing. This will open, balance, and connect all of the chakras together. This can help in spinal adjustments and balancing of yin and yang. Tourmaline appears in many different colors. Which color it is will benefit the corresponding chakra. Red and black tourmaline will help the root chakra, green, pink and watermelon the heart chakra, yellow the solar plexus, and orange the sacral chakra. Natural tourmaline is very popular as is any type of jewelry pieces containing its natural shape. It can also appear tumbled and polished, carved, or cut.

Turquoise
Turquoise has historical significance for many nations, aboriginal tribes, kings, warriors, and shamans. It is a sacred stone of deep healing, power, luck, and protection. It is believed to hold the powers of the heavens balanced with the powers of the earth. It is very popular in jewelry. It relates to the throat chakra, giving voice to creative ideas and personal truth. Turquoise absorbs excessive energy and is a calming and harmonizing stone. Its variation of light blue to deep blue-green turquoise appears naturally, in points or tumbled, and polished.

Zircon

Zircon is a naturally occurring mineral that protects and attracts. It is usually blue or yellow and appears naturally, tumbled and polished, carved, or cut. It is an amplifying crystal that works well with clear quartz and aquamarine. Yellow zircon is associated with the solar plexus chakra and blue zircon with the throat or third eye chakra. It helps with self-love, increasing motivation and enthusiasm for things you may not normally be excited about, creating joy, spiritual growth, connection to the Divine and intuition. You can place zircon on or near the appropriate chakra, as any type of jewelry, especially a necklace or bracelet, at your desk at work or home for when you have tasks that underwhelm you.

Crystal Pairing

Some crystals pair well with others, making them better than the sum of their parts. Crystals that pair well have complementary energies that can really help direct their properties and healing energies. Almost any crystal is amplified when paired with clear quartz. Some other pairings of crystals are described below.

Smoky quartz + Apache tears
This is a powerful combination for people who are grieving. Apache tears help process grief to move forward, while smoky quartz turns negative energy to positive.

Amethyst + Labradorite
This pairing can help you have a more restful night's sleep. Amethyst is a perfect calming stone for insomnia, while labradorite calms nightmares and supports good dreams.

Black Tourmaline + Clear Quartz
This combination balances masculine and feminine energies and can help aid in the free flow of balanced energy.

Citrine + Black Tourmaline
This can help you feel grounded in prosperity. Citrine is a stone of prosperity while black tourmaline is grounding but also blocks negative energy which can help remove thoughts that prevent prosperity.

Rose Quartz + Ruby or Garnet
This pairing is excellent for relationships. Rose quartz is the crystal of unconditional love and supports all kinds of it, as does ruby and garnet. They are also grounding stones which can help keep you grounded while experiencing love and keeping you from losing yourself too much in love.

Crystal Color Guide

Black Crystals
Black crystals absorb light. They are known to show the hidden potential of any situation. Black is grounding and manifesting. It can hold energies safely hidden yet accessible for exploration. Black crystals can have a purifying effect as well. Some black crystals are apache tears, black calcite, hematite, black jade, black jasper, black kyanite, lodestone, obsidian, onyx, black opal, and black tourmaline.

Blue Crystals
Blue crystals are associated with the throat, communication, self-expression, and standing up for yourself. Blue can help in feeling calm and self-assured. Some blue crystals are blue lace agate, blue apatite, aquamarine, blue kyanite, labradorite, lapis lazuli, larimar, sapphire, sodalite, tanzanite, blue tiger's eye, turquoise, blue aventurine, blue calcite, blue chalcedony, and blue fluorite.

Brown Crystals
Brown is associated with the earth, trees, and nature. Brown crystals are known to help with grounding, nurturing, and stabilizing energies. They can help exude warmth, comfort, security, clarity, and balance. Brown agate, brown apatite, amber, bronzite, tiger's eye, and jasper are just a few brown crystals.

Gray Crystals
Gray crystals can be very grounding, protective, and deflective. They will dispel negativity back out into the universe. Gray stones can be helpful in meditation and cleansing. It is also good for overall balancing. Some black crystals include black or gray agate, Botswana agate, gray aventurine, and smoky quartz.

Green Crystals

Green crystals are associated with the heart. They encourage personal space and growth while supporting relationships and balance emotions. Green is also linked to relieving anxiety, calming, good luck, and prosperity. Some green crystals include moss agate, amazonite, green aventurine, green calcite, emerald, epidote, green fluorite, fuchsite, tsavorite garnet, green jade, malachite, moldavite, peridot, green tourmaline, and turquoise.

Orange/Peach Crystals
Orange crystals energize, focus, and allow creativity to flow. It increases motivation, enthusiasm, and basic energy. It can be a warming color as if being the kindling of a fire to get one moving. Orange crystals can benefit the flow of blood in the body supporting organs and tissues. Some orange crystals are orange apatite, orange aventurine, carnelian, hessonite garnet, peach moonstone, fire opal, and padparadscha sapphire.

Red Crystals
Red crystals activate, stimulate, and energize. Associated with the root chakra, red crystals embody practical, everyday survival skills, safety, and security. Red stones are also associated with protection, movement, and motivation. Some red crystals include red agate, red calcite, red garnet, red jade, red Jasper, ruby, and red tiger's eye.

Yellow/Gold Crystals
Yellow crystals relate to the body's nervous, immune, and digestive systems. Stress, fear, contentment, and happiness are all linked to this color. It is also a clearing and focus stone. Some yellow crystals are yellow agate, amber, yellow apatite, yellow aventurine, yellow calcite, citrine, yellow danburite, yellow fluorite, yellow jade, yellow kyanite, yellow tiger's eye, and topaz.

Pink Crystals
Pink crystals have a calming, nurturing, reassuring effect. They have a gentle and subtle way of bringing about a resolution in a compassionate way. They bring sensitivity to daily situations. It will be stated many times that pink is the color of unconditional love. It can also bring to fruition unexpressed feelings of emotion that have been blocking someone from personal growth. Some pink

crystals are pink apatite, pink calcite, pink danburite, pink fluorite, rhodochrosite, rose quartz, and pink tourmaline.

Purple Crystals
Purple or violet is associated with intuition, divinity, imagination, inspiration, and empathy. Purple stones help to rebalance even the most extreme out of balance systems of the body. They are good stress relieving and overall healing stones. The can also be calming, promote lucid dreams, and clarity. Some purple or violet stones are purple agate, amethyst, purple calcite, purple fluorite, and lavender jade.

White/Clear Crystals
White represents clarity, cleansing, and purification. It reflects what is already visible. White and clear are universal energy stones that amplify all other stones, strengthen, and balance. White is also good for healing, manifesting, and during meditation. Some white or clear crystals are white agate, white calcite, danburite, colorless fluorite, howlite, white jade, moonstone, opal, clear quartz, and selenite.

Multicolored Crystals
Multicolored crystals are balancing, grounding, deepen intuition, and promote feelings of love. Multicolored crystals include banded agate, ametrine, rainbow fluorite, and watermelon tourmaline.

CHAPTER 2
Crystals And Healing

Crystals have a long history of healing on many levels. For centuries, societies have valued crystals for their brilliance as precious and semiprecious gemstones as well as for their unique vibrational energies within each crystal that can help facilitate healing for the body, mind, and spirit. Cultures throughout history, including ancient Roman, Greek, Egyptian, and Asian, used crystals for their healing properties. Sacred texts included information about crystal healing, people buried the dead with significant stones, warriors and royalty wore crystals on different parts of their body and made use of talismans and amulets for good luck and protection. Ancient acupuncture needles were tipped with crystals to enhance healing. We find ourselves today utilizing similar techniques involving crystals and healing stones.

History

For a long time, gems, minerals, and crystals have been utilized to achieve physical, emotional, and spiritual wellbeing. Nearly every ancient civilization as described above has used crystals in healing. The history of crystals and healing goes far and wide.

Since the Stone Age, Jade is one of the first mined stones in China. There is a prehistoric monument built on 3,200 BC in Ireland that makes it even older than the pyramids of Egypt and the Stonehenge which is called Newgrange. There is a tomb where the front entrance was built using white quartz cobblestone. Over thousands of years ago, amber beads were found in Britain.

Crystals were a power source in ancient civilizations of Lemuria and Atlantis. The people of Atlantis created patterns with strong energy resources to serve multiple purposes including healing. This is similar to crystal grids we still create and use today.

Ancient Egyptians used many different crystals for a multitude of purposes. Quartz crystals or other gems were placed on the dead's forehead at a funeral. It was believed the energy of the stone would guide the person in the afterlife. Dancers wore crystals, especially carnelian or ruby to appear attractive and support their personal strength. Those of royalty used lapis lazuli which is crushed and placed on the eyes to enhance awareness such as Cleopatra. To promote enlightenment and support the third eye chakra, Pharaohs placed amethysts on their third eye. Clear quartz, carnelian, emerald gems, ruby, turquoise, and lapis lazuli are used for cosmetics and jewelry. For the prevention of wrinkles, Egyptians thought of the use of powdered rose quartz on the face. As for the Priestesses and Priests of Egypt who are also known as healers, they have worn multiple crystals on their bodies. They believed that the gemstones renew their energy and then transmute to those with illness or who needed healing energy.

Mayans used green jade for funeral masks, especially among rulers. They would be buried with the masks believing those in the underworld would recognize them as leaders and treat them well and help them in the underworld. Incans had a belief that the blood of their ancestral rulers is in rhodochrosite. Obsidian weapons were created by the Aztec warriors and used for their strength and grounding energy.

In ancient Chinese culture, green jade was also of high value. The Chinese believed the energy of this crystal promoted prosperity and love. Small and large statues alike have been and continue to be made to symbolize the power of this ancient stone. It reflects the symbol of status, spirituality, health and clarity, and overall good luck.

Greek soldiers would crush hematite that contains iron on them during battle. They thought the energy will give protection as opposed to their opponents. To protect them in battle, as well as to promote health and attraction of good things, Romans wore crystal amulets and talismans. To work against drunkenness, both the Romans and the Greeks used amethyst crystal. This stone was also often used to carve wine goblets.

The healing properties of crystal were documented on Vedas, which is a sacred text in Hinduism. The Kalpa tree which is considered in India as a legendary tree is supposed to be made up of precious stones like topaz, diamond, tiger's eye, ruby, green zircon, coral, emerald, and sapphire.

Virgin Mary, mother to Jesus was symbolized by lapis lazuli in Christianity times. A sapphire from the 12th century is used for the cardinal's ring today.

In Renaissance Europe, healing stones, along with herbal remedies, were used to aid in healing the sick.

For Australia and its native inhabitants, crystals and gemstones have always been given great importance. The commonest is the quartz crystal. It is thought to help connect to the spirits of family and friends who have passed on. A cave that is also believed to house a giant rock quartz crystal is found under the Ayers Rock, Uluru.

In the 1980s, a New Age dawned, creating a resurgence of crystal use, both practical and continued use for healing. Crystal healing continues to grow in popularity today. People, practitioners, and modern healers look back to the historical uses of crystals, gems, and stones and realize their beneficial powers are still the same today. Crystals, including quartz, are even used in a multitude of technological devices such as watches, radios, appliances, computers, and televisions. Western medicine is opening to the effectiveness of alternative therapies such as crystal healing.

Everything is made up of energy. Science has proven all things in the universe have their own frequency and vibration, including crystals. Famous scientists such as Nikola Tesla proved how certain forms of energy can affect the vibrational characteristics of other forms of energy. If you have ever felt the energy sucked right out of you from being around someone who is negative, or felt extremely happy around someone who is upbeat, this is what it feels like to be aligned or entrained by others' energy fields. This can apply to crystals as well, as they too have energy levels. The vibrational energy within crystals affects the energy fields all around them, including the human energy field. How this helps in healing is that crystals usually have a higher vibrational frequency than subtle human body fields. If we use crystals on or around our energy field, we can then take on that higher vibration of the crystal. We will start to feel lighter, brighter, on a higher frequency than before we began to work with crystals. Crystals do not actually do the healing themselves. They vibrate a certain energy that your body aligns with and you do the healing by taking in that energy. Our bodies then naturally take that higher energy and adjust to that for whatever needs necessary at the moment, instead of any negative or heavier energy that may be causing a blockage or disease. Vibrating at a higher rate is helpful to humans because it helps us advance spiritually and move in more positive directions physically, mentally, and emotionally. We learn to heal from within, naturally. This type of healing occurs gently and non-invasively yet is very self-empowering.

Healing must take place on all levels to fully initiate and complete the healing circle. It is not enough to treat any disease or illness only on the physical level as this would only treat the symptoms. This is the common western way of medical treatment. The root of the disease must be found and treated on the soul or spiritual level in order to completely heal with permanent results. Many natural healers believe we are here on earth for soul growth. This occurs through our body's natural healing abilities and powers. Crystal healing can be viewed as certainly promoting this type of development on the physical, emotional, mental, and spiritual levels. Practitioners of natural healing are re-discovering this ancient healing modality.

Crystals are natural elements that come from the earth. They can help us feel grounded. They can also help us connect to our energetic selves, the subtle energy bodies existing outside our physical one. This includes our aura, etheric body or biomagnetic sheath, as well as our higher self and Divinity. This helps us keep balance with spirit and our physical, emotional, and mental wellbeing. Humans exist only with all of these levels. Crystals support this existence in a positive way. When choosing a crystal to work with, let its color, feel, vibration, all come into play. Let it resonate without judgment. Sometimes you will just know when a crystal looks or feels right.

Holistic Healing

One way to use crystals in healing on all Physical, Emotional, Mental, Spiritual (PEMS) levels is through meditation. This will be discussed more specifically in Chapter 7. When we meditate, we are focusing on the present very intently. When we introduce the healing work of a crystal into this practice, we enhance the benefits greatly! Meditating allows us to be still, present, repeat a positive affirmation. This intention or mantra connects us to our higher selves and a higher vibration. Since crystals generally have higher vibrations, they are a natural enhancement to meditation practice. When we focus our intentions while gazing at or holding a specific crystal, this increases the power of the energy and intention. You may not feel something right away. Be patient, open-minded, and keep trying.

A thoughtfully considered intention is the starting point for healing with crystals. Specific intentions instilled into daily thought patterns also become part of its energy. We always have free will to choose our thoughts as each day brings forth new challenges and wonderful beginnings. Healing crystals help us focus our intention, quiet our mind, and reconnect to the universally healing vibrations of the Earth.

Thoughts create vibrations throughout the universe, which makes setting intentions a powerful way to achieve happiness and wellbeing. Having a clear purpose provides us with insight into our dreams, aspirations, and values. It also helps us to be in the present instead of being caught in negative thought patterns. We can also get stuck in past patterns that have never or no longer serve us in any way positively. Crystals can help alleviate these doubts. Intentions are like magnets by attracting what can make them come true. Creating an intention starts by setting goals that align with your values, aspiration, and purpose.

Healing the body
Your body is the physical part of you. Crystals can help balance bodily energies and facilitate physical change. This could include relieving headaches, exhaustion, fatigue, joint, or muscle pain. Crystals can even help with such physical ailments as seasonal allergies, sore throats, and fevers. They should, however, never substitute care from a qualified healthcare provider.

Healing the mind

Your mind is both physical and nonphysical. The physical aspects of your mind include the brain and nervous system. The nonphysical aspects include emotions, thoughts, and dreams. The vibration in crystals can help balance energies of the mind to bring about healing. Conditions that can be eased might include emotional issues, stress, anxiety, insomnia, nightmares, depression, and grief.

Healing your spirit

Your spirit is purely a nonphysical part of you. Crystals can assist in balancing spiritual energies such as unconditional love, forgiveness, compassion, and belief systems. They can also facilitate communication with your higher self and a higher power.

Health benefits

When crystals are carried, worn, held, or even just gazed at or placed in a meaningful area, they have an added benefit to our subtle energies surrounding our physical body.

Chakras linked the subtle bodies to the physical body or centers that mediate and circulate energy. Using crystals in our daily lives this way can help create balance, stability, peace, and joy.

Increase energy

Many specific crystals can be used to increase energy. Red and orange ones are excellent for overcoming energy depletion. They not only boost energy but they also help to get positive thoughts flowing again while getting rid of negativity. From long ago to now, it is said to be beneficial to wear a red crystal or amulet to help purify the blood and allow it to flow freely. When blood flows clear and free, our life force or Qi is strong! Vitality is strong and we feel driven, have a purpose.

Crystals which are red and orange are commonly known to give motivation and energy. Orange carnelian, red jasper, ruby, and bloodstone are fine examples of crystals that are associated with stimulation while providing balance. Carnelian can be carried for an instant pick me up. Simply holding it for a few minutes can improve your energy levels. Red Jasper can be used longer term, holding a long storage of energy when needed. It can help to place this on any lower chakras when you need a boost of lasting energy or have been exhausted over time.

Clear quartz is a master energizer for the aura or biomagnetic sheath. Energizing your aura has an overall beneficial effect on your energy level in general, but it also makes your physical body feel more energetic. Placing a clear quartz crystal over your body, just below your navel for ten to fifteen minutes can help you feel recharged and ready for anything.

Clear the Mind
Crystals are powerful in stimulating a lethargic mind and promotes calmness as well. Crystal can assist in boosting a person's creativity, clarity, and concentration. They help raise human vibration thus bringing focus to your mind. Crystals to use for mind calming and clearing are clear quartz, amethyst, sodalite, bloodstone, and carnelian.

Clear quartz placed above or around the head and crown chakra will provide your body with clearing energy and allow it to get back to its most perfect state of balance. Calming amethyst relaxes your mind and improves your memory, creating focus and concentration. Carnelian can be very activating, letting the mind sharply focus, and dismiss mental fogginess. Sodalite also has a strong effect on the mind. It can eliminate mental confusion and encourage intuitive perception and reasonable thought. This opens the mind to see things in a different manner and to receive useful new information. Bloodstone can be an excellent tonic crystal to relieve an overactive mind. It reduces mental confusion while increasing alertness. It helps in adapting to changing or stressful situations, maintaining mental stability. This helps in clear decision-making. It can be beneficial to keep a bloodstone in your pocket during any type of test or exam, to help focus on a solution rather than a problem.

Creativity
By uniting the right and left hemispheres of your brain, the capacity to solve problems and creativity can be expanded. The right side is more intuitive, creative, and willing to take risks. The left side of the brain is analytical, logical, and fact-based. Crystals can bridge the gap between the two and channel their powers.

Crystals are able to assist and help when you feel burned out and your creative paths feel stuck. Red and orange crystals such as carnelian, red or even yellow Jasper are warming and stimulating stones. They can be used to stimulate creativity and boost self-esteem with their vibrant colors. You will be able to reach your goals and confidently move forward as they increase passion and motivation. Carnelian, in particular, is considered a strong action stone.

Red or yellow Jasper helps you realize a problem assertively. They combine organization (think compartmentalization) with imagination. Red Jasper, in particular, can bring forth conflict before it becomes too overwhelming. It allows you to investigate new coping strategies and provides useful insight into the most difficult situations. Both red and yellow Jasper increases creativity.

Healing sessions

Crystal healing therapy has been used for over 5,000 years but still continues today, especially in Ayurvedic Medicine from India and Traditional Chinese Medicine or TCM. Practitioners have studied past uses of the therapy to become knowledgeable about the techniques in order to apply them to modern illnesses and disease.

This book will help you collect and work with crystals on your own. However, it is important to know how a healing session with a practitioner may be, or if you would like to emulate your own healing session in the comfort of your own home. Healers who use crystals believe the stones work as conduits to attract positive energy into the body while drawing negative energy away from it. Neither the practitioner nor the crystals are doing the actual healing. It is up to the person receiving it to be open to this natural modality in order to allow the healing to occur within them. It has been discussed previously how this can help keep all levels of energy balanced, from the physical, emotional, mental, and spiritual aspects. Indeed crystal healing is a gentle yet powerful way to heal!

One way a crystal healer may perform a session is to have you first fill out an informational form regarding past and current issues and background. They may have you sit or lie comfortably on a therapy table or even on the floor. Your chakras will be assessed to see where attention is needed. Appropriate crystals will be used to open, cleanse, and balance the major chakras. Usually, a specific crystal layout will be determined for individual needs and placed on and around the body. They will be activated to their fullest healing potential to promote healing and restore balance. There may be soothing music, sound therapy, and essential oils used. The receiver should be deeply relaxed during the session and rejuvenated afterward. Anything that is felt after a session is deemed appropriate as we all react differently to healing. You may feel tired or anxious as you release some no longer needed energy. Overall, you should have a complete feeling of wellbeing. Never does crystal therapy replace medical attention from a traditional medical doctor, nor does it claim to cure any illness.

What to Expect
When energy healing work is done, the energy will align with your highest and greatest good. Sometimes the change you think you need or want is not what best serves you. Get rid of any expectation of the result and allow what serves you to come forth. When we set expectations and stick to them, we limit ourselves and results. What we imagine is usually smaller than what the universe makes available to us. Sometimes what serves our greatest good doesn't appear as we think it should.

Try to remove "should" and "could" from your vocabulary and accept what the energy brings. Sometimes changes are subtle and take a while to occur. Sometimes they are immediate and very obvious. Oftentimes, when major healing occurs, a shift in our reality can throw us completely off balance. Understand the need for change but allow yourself to let go of any expectations of how and what change should happen. Set your intention, do the work, remove judgment and expectation, and be open. The energy will always serve your greater good.

Crystals and the Moon
A new and a full moon are very sacred times full of energy. The full moon reflects the outcome of both your physical work and your energetic manifestations. To utilize this energetic, sacred time to your advantage, a full or new moon ritual is a powerful way to harness the energy and to magnify it positively to benefit your life and higher self. Whether you choose to celebrate the full or new

moon with an elaborate ritual, a brief meditation or any other personal technique, introducing healing crystals into this practice will increase and strengthen your manifestation abilities. Working with crystals in this way strengthens them for that moon cycle, as well as the one immediately following.

There are particular crystals that will work most effectively during the full or new moon phase. The ones you pick for use are usually uniquely personal choices based on what you relate to the best. You can very clearly state intentions between the phases of the moon. The new moon is actually a wonderfully magical time to set intentions. By the time the full moon has arrived, it is believed your intentions set will come to fruition. When the full moon does arrive, it is good to reflect on any gifts received and express gratitude. This is often a time for deep introspection. What can you do to better yourself, your life, grow physically, mentally, and spiritually? The energy of the full moon is always positive. It is thought to be feminine, goddess-like. This means it relates to the psychic, mysterious, softer yet cooler aspect of our selves. The moon is feminine yin and dark, to the masculine yang and light of the sun.

Using crystals and their unique powers during the phases of the moon can increase what you create to be even more abundant. If you are satisfied with your status quo and ask for that to stay the same, use this energetic time with your crystals to be grateful and expand your gratitude for what you have. Always live in gratitude. With the next moon phase, you can state a new intention including any growth you may have experienced. Let go of whatever you need to let go of and let the powers of the crystals and moon expand the positive aspects of the whole experience.

When working with different phases of the moon, your genuine intention and working with that particular moon phase is more relevant than the specific crystals you choose to work with. There are a number of crystals that have vibrational frequencies that align with the moon in general, no matter what phase it is in at that particular time.

Even though the moon really represents feminine energy, it does embody both yin and yang, like our own bodies. The moon is balanced in itself. The full moon is thought to be masculine, yang energy, a time for action and completion. The intentions or seeds we plant at the time of the new moon are now in full swing and must be acted upon. The new moon is more introspective, about going within. It is feminine, yin energy, a time to gratefully express desired intentions. New moon energy requires more thoughtful action with our minds and spirit. We can meditate quietly yet be acutely aware of any messages we receive in order to help us set objectives.

Selenite
Selenite is a beautiful, soft white crystal that can be iridescent and reminiscent of the moon and its glow. This crystal can be beneficial for letting go or for setting forth action. It is a highly protective and amplifying crystal. This makes it quite perfect for setting intentions during phases of the moon. It is very unique and powerful in that it does not need to be cleansed as it does not absorb or store energy. It serves as a clearing stone for other crystals because of this quality. It readily protects against negativity. Selenite also helps with clearing your aura, increasing intuition, and connecting with your higher self and divinity. Selenite is a good crystal to work with when wishing to work with forgiveness and the moon phases. During the full moon, selenite can be receptive of its abundantly available bounty and clear blockages to help you let go of anything that no longer serves you. It will rejuvenate you and recharge your energy field and chakras, to help you step into the next moon phase with your full potential.

Moonstone
Any type or color of moonstone is terrific for working with lunar energy at any moon phase. Its basic coloring is a milky grey, peach or white with an opalescent sheen. It is known for its protectiveness, connecting to higher realms, divinity, and intuition. Moonstone is also helpful during water or night time travel. These characteristics make it a perfect crystal to use in working with the phases of the moon.

Labradorite
Labradorite is another wonderful choice to work with moon energy. It is a protective crystal associated with magic. It can help open your third eye chakra, thus allow you to be receptive to receive

from higher realms and your higher self. It is beneficial to increasing intuition. It reduces negativity and dispels illusion. This can help in setting realistic yet mystical intentions during the moon phases.

Usage

There are a number of different ways to use any of the above crystals during new or full moon phases. You can place the crystal under your pillow during the night of a full or new moon. This can help release the power of the moon in your dreams and cause you to have very vivid dreams with intuitive messages. You can also place a crystal or group of crystals in the full moonlight for charging. Clearly state the intention you wish these stones to amplify. Ask that they carry that energy into the next moon phases. On the day of a full or new moon, carry a crystal of your choice with you. It will serve as a reminder of your intentions, work to be done, letting go, as you are in tune with that powerful moon phase throughout the day. During a new or full moon ritual or meditation, keep a crystal of choice near you or in your hands. This will enhance the moon's powerful energy of this phase and allow you to go deeper into your practice.

Grounding

When working with the powerful phases of the moon, it is easy to become overwhelmed or imbalanced. To help with this, it is important to have a grounding crystal readily available. Good grounding stones are smoky quartz, black tourmaline, and hematite.

CHAPTER 3
Creating Crystal Grids

A crystal grid is the formation of different crystals with the intention of creating powerful energy focused on a specific intent. Grids can be simple or complex. A crystal grid is the combined energy of the crystals you use, the layout you create, and the intention you set. You should intent what you need, not necessarily what you think you want. Once you decide which crystals you would like to use in your grid, you can choose or create a shape. You can certainly make your grid in any shape and include any extras such as tree branches or bark, leaves, flowers, candles, etc., but some find using basic sacred geometric shapes enhance the power of the grid. Spirals represent the pathway to consciousness. Circles signify continual rebirth, unity, and growth. The infinity symbol represents endlessness and dates back to 1655. Squares represent earthly elements. Triangles or pyramids are connected to divinity and represent the connection between body, mind, and spirit.

To use a grid, create it anywhere it will be most beneficial such as under your bed or on your desk or sacred space. You will be able to set the intent and keep the grid there over time. Write an intention on a piece of paper to include under the center crystal. This should be an intent we truly need rather than just a want. The universe will only give us what we are ready to handle.

To arrange your grid, there should be a focus stone in the center or middle of the grid. This is the primary energy you are trying to attain. The surrounding stones enhance the energy, allowing it to move outward from the focus. Outer stones can either be the source of intention for the primary energy, or they can be a perimeter stone to keep the energy within the grid.

Choose your crystals based on specific need, your intuition, as well as what you have readily available to you. Clear the crystals and space you will create your grid by burning sage, incense, or singing bowls. You can also clear crystals using water, moonlight, or by burying in the earth for the amount of time that feels right. Be aware of the crystal's properties when clearing them. Some do not like water or to be in the ground very long.

Put your intention you wrote on a piece of paper in the center of the grid under the center crystal point. You may state your intention out loud or silently. Take a few deep breaths before-hand and be aware of slowing down, mindful of your breath and clearing your mind. Allow your intention to resonate within you and your crystals and grid. Place the rest of the crystals in whatever shape you feel drawn to. Using a crystal quartz or whatever point you choose, start to activate your grid. You can go from the inside out or outside in. Touch each crystal with your starter point and create an invisible line connecting each crystal to each other, keeping in mind your true intention. When finished touching each crystal point to point, take a few more deep breaths. Thank the universe and Divine for allowing your intentions to be heard. With gratitude, keep your grid up for at least 48 hours or more or whatever time frame feels right for you.

Grid for abuse
Create a crystal grid that helps with three major issues that often may arise from abuse — security, self-esteem, and personal strength. Use a triangle grid that balances body, mind, and spirit. Place the grid anywhere where you usually are such as near the bed and desk. Cleanse the crystals about once a month. Any size or shape of stone will work as long as it feels right to you.

Use black tourmaline as the main focus stone for safety, security, and absorbing negative energy. The intention stones could be citrine for self-esteem and power, rose quartz for self-love, carnelian for personal power and activation. Perimeter stones should be clear quartz to enhance all the other stones.

Anger release grid
Use a basic circular grid for unity and oneness. The stones in this grid are designed to do two things — absorb the anger and increase compassion. Place it anywhere you spend a lot of time or under your bed. Cleanse the stones, particularly the focus stone every few days. Any shape or form of stone will work here.

Courage grid

Amazonite is a good crystal to use to promote courage. Create a square courage grid using aquamarine and citrine above and below with amazonite as the focus or center stone and quartz points as perimeter stones to direct and amplify the energy. Place the courage grid anywhere you spend a lot of time and can reflect upon.

Intuition/Psychic grid

Make a third eye grid with amethyst and clear quartz to stimulate your intuition and psychic abilities. You can create the grid as an actual eye shape with amethyst in the center. Lay it out on your bedside table, state your question or intention before you go to sleep, then sleep on it. The amethyst and clear quartz will help the answer come to you as you are asleep.

Forgiveness grid

Using a spiral shape with Selenite as the center focus stone and clear quartz as all other points on the grid, create a forgiveness grid. Place it where you can meditate on it easily and comfortably. Sit or lie near the grid and visualize the person you wish to forgive. Imagine both of you connected together energetically as physical ties between you. Then imagine cutting those ties as you repeat a mantra such as, "I release you." Once the ties are cut, visualize the person you need to forgive surrounded in white light. This can be a very powerful release and may cause strong emotions to flow. Allow them to be released from you. Forgiveness is not always about the other person but rather allowing yourself to forgive and move on. It is not always easy. State your forgiveness intention clearly and truthfully and amazing letting go will occur.

Gratitude grid

Living with gratitude can be such a wonderful, humbling experience. It allows you to align with who you truly are and what really matters in life. A gratitude grid can help amplify all the goodness that surrounds us as humans. Create a heart-shaped grid where you can easily and comfortably meditate. Use rose quartz as the center focus stone, preferably heart-shaped if you have it! Clear quartz should be the amplifying perimeter stones as the outline of the heart. Sit near the grid and close your eyes. Visualize gratitude flowing through your body and into your heart and imagine your heart delivering gratitude throughout your entire body. Allow the gratitude to flow through and around you. When you live with gratitude, real change can occur for you.

Grief grid
Grief is the natural feeling of loss and is necessary to experience in order to move forward. If we get stuck in grief at any point, crystal healing can help facilitate removing of blockages to pass through the sadness and again experience joy. A grief grid can help speed the process along if we are stuck for too long. Make a stage of grief grid and place it somewhere you spend a lot of time.

Place the stones in a spiral with an Apache tear as the center stone with the following stones spiraling outward — hematite for anger, rainbow fluorite for denial, blue kyanite for bargaining, smoky quartz for depression, and amethyst for acceptance. There really isn't a focus stone or perimeter stone as each stone in the grief grid helps you manage one stage of grief at a time. Working with this grid helps you feel love again, release, and heal pain.

Peace grid
There is a Serenity Prayer that creates a path to peace — changing what you can control and letting go of what you cannot, and understanding the difference between the two. A peace grid can help you feel peace in even the most challenging of times because it helps you let go and overcome the urge to control. It helps us experience inner peace and wisdom.

Shape a circle grid for oneness and unity with turquoise as the center focus stone representing inner peace. The first circle around the turquoise should be aquamarine for letting go and another circle after that with amethyst to represent good judgment.

Regret grid
Regret is a strong emotion that can keep us focused on negative past circumstances instead of the current, more positive present conditions we are living in the here and now. It can be a big cause of situational disease or long-term illness by holding on to past regret. Self-forgiveness is crucial in overcoming regret. A grid to release regret using crystals can be very beneficial.

To create a grid for releasing regret, place it on a flat surface in which you usually stay. Use a triangle shape to connect body, mind, and spirit. The main center focus stone should be a smoky quartz to release old belief systems and transform negative to positive. The middle intention stones should be aquamarine which helps release old patterns. The perimeter stones of protection should be black tourmaline which absorbs negativity. It can help to repeat the mantra "I separate and forgive myself from my regrets of the past," while confirming your intention in a grid to release regret.

Rejection grid
As will be stated in further chapters, we have no control over whether somebody wants us, likes us, or chooses us, but that doesn't stop it from hurting when rejection does occur. To heal the pain from rejection, you must return to a place of self-love. Rose quartz is extremely effective for this. It is the stone for unconditional love and will bring you back to that space. Rhodonite is also a good stone for dealing with loss and rejection. It is often used to prevent injury and loss, thus can be seen as a protection and insurance type crystal. Any pink, green, or vibrantly colored orange or even yellow crystal can help with the lower chakras and heart chakra. When these are open, balanced, and functioning optimally, you will feel safe, grounded, protected, yet have a strong sense of self and self-worth. These qualities will help you feel safe from rejection and have the courage to keep opportunities available. Carnelian is a bright orange crystal that aids in overcoming abuse of any kind in order to trust yourself and others again. It can help dispel envy and rage. These crystals will also help in dealing with recovery from any rejection or abandonment in the future. Use a triangle shaped grid to connect body, mind, and spirit. Have the main center focus stone be rose quartz or rhodonite to accentuate self-love. Use the other crystals mentioned in a pattern you intuitively arrange. There is no right or wrong placement of the crystals. Repeat the mantra, "I trust myself and know I am always worthy of true love" while affirming your intention in a rejection grid.

Prosperity grid
Learning to be grateful for what we do have is key to feeling an abundance of prosperity. We often do not lack as much as we think we do. When we begin to focus on the positive, what we do have,

instead of the negative, what we think we want, we then begin to live a light, prosperous life.

To create a prosperity grid, place it in your home's prosperity corner, or the back left corner of where you spend the most time daily. Create a square with infinity symbol in the center of it or the creation shape. The center focus stone should be citrine for prosperity. The crystals along the middle infinity symbol should be turquoise to represent luck and prosperity. The perimeter square stones should be clear quartz to amplify all the other crystals and intentions. Repeat the mantra "I am thankful I am prosperous."

Crystal grids can work wonders to fulfill positive intentions. They can help us let go and fill our daily lives with balance and fullness. You can complete a crystal grid whenever you feel the need to, but a new moon or a full moon is an excellent time energetically to do a grid. Using the powers of mother nature, where crystals originate and feel right at home in, can only enhance the healing capabilities of all crystals and stones. We are at our best when we are one with nature. Crystals let us know this whenever we allow them to help us heal. You can use any of the grids described in this chapter or feel free to create your own individualized grid and intention.

CHAPTER 4
Crystals And Chakras

Chakras are energy centers that connect your physical body to your subtle bodies that surround your physical body in your biomagnetic sheath or aura. Your chakras connect your body to the energy of your mind and spirit. Chakras distribute life force, vitality, Qi, through the physical and subtle bodies. Many energy workers, practitioners, and healers count 12 main chakras. Some count even more up to 114 of them, including major, minor, and micro chakras! Your seven main chakras, the ones focused on in this book, run along your spinal column. Each main chakra is associated with a specific color that corresponds to various energies that govern different aspects of human emotion and behavior. Imbalances in the chakras may correlate to physical, emotional, mental, or spiritual issues. Diseases and conflicts on the physical, emotional, mental, or spiritual level occur and the flow of subtle energy becomes imbalanced when chakras are blocked.

To help balance these energies, you can work with crystals by placing similarly colored ones on corresponding chakras.

Chakras create a state of harmony or disharmony depending on how well each one is functioning. Keeping them cleansed, balanced, and recharged is important for holistic healing and wellbeing. There are techniques in which crystals can help with this. If you have physical, emotional, mental, or spiritual issues connected to a specific chakra, your health and wellbeing will benefit by placing the crystal on the chakra and keeping it there for 20 minutes or longer while relaxing quietly. Certain issues correspond with the chakras and each chakra has a different color associated with it. Other energies are also associated with colors, so choosing crystals with those colors can help you work through particular issues.

Root Chakra - The first and the root chakra is located at the seat or base of your spine and vibrates red. It is the center associated with survival instincts and relates to safety and security issues as well as issues of the legs, feet, and hips. Family and tribal/community identity have to do with the root chakra. Some positive qualities associated with the root chakra are basic security, sense of one's own power, mobility, independence, and leadership. Some negative or shadow aspects of this chakra are impatience, fear, vengeance, anger, violence, overactive, manipulative. The root chakra links distinctively to the physical body.

Red is equal to grounding, passion, vitality, physical energy, and stability. Crystals good for the root chakra vibrating red are red jasper, garnet, ruby, hematite, smoky quartz, red zincite, black tourmaline, and black obsidian.

Sacral Chakra - The sacral and second chakra is located right below your navel area and vibrates orange. It is the source of creativity, personal power, prosperity, and procreation. Issues related to the sacral chakra are digestive, abdominal, lower back, and sexual organ issues. Positive aspects are assertiveness, confidence, joy, sensuality, fertility, and acceptance of sexual identity. Shadow qualities include low self-esteem, infertility, sluggishness, inferiority, arrogance, and emotional hurdles or blockages. The sacral chakra connects the physical body.

Orange is associated with self-identity, sexuality, family issues, ego, and social anxiety. Crystals that benefit the sacral chakra are orange carnelian, orange calcite, turquoise, and fluorite.

Solar Plexus Chakra - The solar plexus and third chakra are right below your sternum and above your navel, vibrates yellow, and is related to boundaries and self-esteem. Physical issues are often related to the lower mid-back, pancreas, spleen, gallbladder, and urinary system. Some positive qualities of the solar plexus chakra are organization, logic, intelligence, empathy, and good use of energy. Negative qualities include overly emotional, lethargic, poor use of energy, cynical, emotional baggage, energy leakage, and taking on other's feelings and problems. The solar plexus chakra is linked to the emotional level.

Yellow relates to self-worth, self-esteem, self-love, and identity. Yellow jasper, citrine, amber, and golden calcite are good crystals for this chakra.

Heart Chakra - The heart and fourth chakra is located in the center of your chest and vibrates green related to compassion, unconditional love, kindness, nurturing, accepting, generosity, and forgiveness. Shadow qualities include jealousy, possessiveness, unable to demonstrate love, disconnected from feelings, insecure, and resistant to change. Issues associated with the heart chakra are physical ones relating to ribs, lungs, and heart. Grief can take a toll on the heart chakra. This chakra links to the emotional level.

Green is associated with love, finances, wealth, forgiveness, and compassion. Crystals that benefit the heart chakra are rose quartz, watermelon tourmaline, green aventurine, and jade.

Throat Chakra - The throat and fifth chakra is in the center of your throat and vibrates blue. It is related to speaking your truth and letting go of personal will to allow in Divine guidance. Positive attributes are being loyal, receptive, a good communicator, and idealistic. Shadow qualities are being unable to speak about thoughts or feelings, being stuck, inflexible, and disloyal. Physical issues include thyroid, throat, and mouth. The throat chakra links the emotional to the mental level.

Blue exudes truth, wisdom, loyalty, and listening. Crystals that help the throat chakra are sodalite, blue calcite, blue chalcedony, blue calcite, amazonite, blue turquoise, and aquamarine.

Third Eye Chakra - The sixth chakra or known as the third eye or brow chakra sits directly in the center of your forehead. This chakra vibrates indigo and corresponds to intuition and intellect. Positive qualities consist of being intuitive, perceptive, visionary, and in the present. Negative qualities are being fearful, attached to the past, superstitious, and overwhelmed with the thoughts of others. Physical issues include eyes, ears, head, and brain. The third eye chakra is linked to the mental level.

Indigo represents spirituality, psychic power, and intuition. Beneficial crystals include lapis lazuli, azurite, tanzanite, and sodalite.

Crown Chakra - The seventh chakra or the crown chakra sits at the top of your head. It vibrates violet purple. The crown chakra corresponds with your higher self and Divinity. Positive qualities include being mystical, creative, and humanitarian. Negative aspects are controlling, illusory, arrogant, and overly-imaginative. Systemic issues and musculoskeletal issues are related to the crown chakra. It links to the spiritual level.

Purple is associated with universal consciousness, energy, perfection, and enlightenment. Crystals to use with your crown chakra include amethyst, quartz crystal, white topaz, selenite, and Herkimer diamond.

Cleansing and Recharging Chakras with Crystals

Intuitive healers can see or feel healthy spinning chakras as colorful, bright light wheels. They spin vibrantly and completely. When they see gray, dull, or black sections, or unsteady spinning of chakra wheels, this signifies imbalance or physical, emotional, mental, or spiritual disease. When using crystals to heal yourself, it isn't even necessary to be able to see the chakras spinning or not. A crystal will attune to any imbalance, bring re-energize the chakra and bring it back to harmony. It is beneficial to do a whole chakras cleanse for a full adjustment. You could cleanse just one or two if you identify with an illness associated with that particular chakra such those described earlier.

Full Chakra Cleanse
For a full chakra cleanse, balance and recharge, you can follow these steps, using the appropriate crystals:

Lie down in a comfortable position. As you place each crystal as described below, imagine an energy and light that is radiating from the crystal for a couple of minutes.
You should be mindful that the chakra's spin is regulated and it is in the process of being cleansed.

On the earth chakra, put the smoky quartz slightly below and between your feet.
On the root chakra, put the red jasper.
On the sacral chakra, put the orange carnelian.
On the solar plexus chakra, put the yellow jasper.

On the heart chakra, put a green aventurine.
On the throat chakra, put the blue lace agate.
On the brow or third eye chakra, put a sodalite.
On the crown chakra, put an amethyst.

Now, slowly turn your focus on the soles of your feet up to the body's middle part. Feel how more balanced and harmonized each chakra has become.

Relax, taking deep breaths downward in the abdomen then hold and count to seven before exhaling. When you inhale and hold off for a while, feel the crystal's energy re-energizing your chakras. You should be able to experience the chakras radiating vibrantly through you from there.

If you are done and you are ready, collect the crystals and you should start on the crown chakra. Be aware of a grounding cord anchoring you to the earth and to your physical body as you are reaching the earth chakra.

After using the crystals, you should cleanse them.

Activating Higher Chakras
Include all crystals as described for the full chakra cleanse layout. In addition, you will be using bloodstone, rose quartz, labradorite, and clear quartz. You may need some assistance laying out all of the crystals on and around you.

Hold all 12 crystals in your hands for a few minutes, visualizing them bathed in bright white light. Lay out each crystal as described for Full Chakra Cleanse. In addition to the eight crystals in a full chakra cleanse, for activating higher chakras, you will need to:

Place bloodstone about 30 cm or 12 inches below your feet.
Place rose quartz three fingers width above your heart.
Place labradorite 15 cm or six inches above your head.
Place clear quartz 30 cm or 12 inches above your crown.

With all 12 crystals in place, draw your attention down to the bloodstone and be mindful of the higher earth chakra opening. Feel how it pulls refined earth energies in and radiates them up to the smoky quartz and through your whole body. Be aware of your connection to the earth's biomagnetic sheath or aura. Feel yourself aligning to the faster and lighter vibration that it carries and how it connects to the lower chakras.

Take your attention up to the rose quartz. Feel how the higher heart chakra opens and expands, receiving and radiating unconditional love as it activates your innate compassion and connection with others. Feel how this chakra connects to the throat chakra so you can communicate love out to the world.

Finally, take your attention up to the clear quartz above your head. Be aware of its connection to higher spiritual guidance. Feel how the energy flows down into the labradorite, activating its hidden awareness and soul memory. Recognize that you are a spiritual being on a human journey!

When the activation is finished, slowly remove the crystals starting with the highest crown chakra, working down to the earth chakra. When you reach the earth chakra, again be mindful of the grounding cord linking your feet to this chakra, grounding you within your physical body to the earth. After you pick up the bloodstone from the higher earth chakra, stand up and feel your feet firmly on the ground. Repeat this higher chakra exercise daily until activation is complete.
In addition to chakra cleansing and activation with crystals, many people wear crystal jewelry corresponding to the main chakras connected to the physical body. You can wear the rainbow of chakra related colors or one of the colors corresponding to a chakra that needs extra support. For example, wear a red Jasper bracelet to support your root chakra. Wear a green aventurine necklace to help activate your heart chakra.

Crystals can be very powerful healing tools in cleansing and activating chakras.

CHAPTER 5
Crystals In Reiki

Reiki is a great, holistic procedure used to relieve stress and develop good overall feelings of wellbeing. It is also known to promote relaxation. It can also be an extraordinary healing modality. Even though each experience will be uniquely felt, most people report feeling extremely safe, warm, radiant, and filled with peace and calm. Some have even left a session completely rid of their disease or concern they came in with.

Thoughts create vibrations within the universe. This makes setting intentions a powerful instrument in achieving feelings of joy and wellbeing. Intentions are like magnets. They can attract what will make them come true, as in the law of attraction. Setting healing intentions with the use of crystals is even more powerful. Crystals vibrate with universal bright light. Having them absorb and work with positive human intentions adds to their usefulness and make them all the more powerful. Reiki, or spiritually guided life force energy, allows a body to learn to heal naturally. Combined with crystal use, these two gentle healing modalities enhance health and wellbeing on all levels powerfully. Reiki and crystal healing allow the physical body to be balanced and healthy by touching the subtle bodies. Healing then occurs on the physical, emotional, mental, and spiritual level.

Reiki is a non-invasive and gentle healing modality that enhances the body's natural healing abilities by utilizing universal life energy. Reiki is derived from two words – Rei or the Higher Power, and Ki or Life Force Energy. A session of Reiki, along with the healing power of crystals, results in an amazing, mutual healing experience. Energy blockages and stagnation are cleared easily with this potent pairing. The receiver will feel lighter, refreshed, centered, and relaxed.

A Reiki crystal healing session is similar to a traditional Reiki session, with the addition of carefully chosen crystals. The client lies with his clothes on and comfortably on a treatment table. The hands of the Reiki practitioner are placed and moved over the client's body by either very lightly touching or just above. This placement and movement of hands allows the Reiki energy to flow in and around the client's body. In a Reiki crystal session, precise crystals are placed on the body, usually on or around a chakra center. The addition of the crystals to the Reiki session enhances and amplifies the healing power of the Reiki energy. The practitioner becomes a mode of transportation for Reiki energy to flow through, to be received by the client where it is needed most. Crystals can help speed up the healing process of a Reiki session.

Before any Reiki session with crystals, the healing room or area should be cleared energetically. This can be done using clear quartz points or really any crystal that feels right. You or the practitioner can channel Reiki energy, positive intention, through the crystals or Reiki symbols to clear the room and protect it.

When a client arrives for a session for the first time, they fill out a health background questionnaire. This helps the practitioner figure out precisely the issues of concern that need to be addressed for that session. Crystals are carefully chosen and placed on and around the client. Some crystals may be chosen to help a client who may feel particularly anxious or nervous about the session. They may be placed under the client. A full body Reiki treatment is conducted with the crystals in place. All of this is done peacefully and gently. They may be re-arranged during a session, according to the practitioner's intuition, spiritual, or Reiki guidance. The session ends with the removal of the crystals and checking of client's chakras for optimal balance and function. Gratitude should be expressed to the spiritual energies as well as to the crystals. Information is shared, questions asked, and good energy felt from combined Reiki and crystal earth elements. The client may receive a Crystal Prescription on how to use prescribed crystals for further healing at home.

Reiki is truly a special healing. Crystals certainly enhance this unique experience.

CHAPTER 6
Clearing And Protection With Crystals

It has been stated before and will be again, when you feel that you want to wear or have a particular crystal, subconsciously, you can be expressing a need for its protective vibrations. Vibrations of crystals are great for counteracting all kinds of negative energy. Negative energies are lightly repelled, excess energies are alleviated, and toxicity is absorbed, thus providing harmony in the home, office, or any surroundings. They also create harmony within the self. Where would we be without these light energy workers?

Crystal Protection

There is an overabundance of negative energy out there in the world. Several crystals are extremely efficient in protecting against someone with negative intentions toward you, or from those who drain energy away from you. Many crystals also dispel other people's negative attitudes or emotions such as jealousy and envy that may harmfully affect you. Those who are sensitive very often feel the pull if anyone is drawing on their energy. Placing yellow jasper over your solar plexus can protect you against this. If you are a main attraction for ill-wishing, wear amethyst or labradorite around your neck for protection.

Energy vampirism happens when someone feeds off your own energy. A soft kind of this vampirism can happen through the spleen. If anyone is strongly attached to you or is vigorously draining your energy, you may feel fatigued or have a pain below your left armpit area when in contact with a particular person. Green aventurine crystal will protect your spleen and rejuvenate your energy. You can also use a spleen protection pyramid to protect your energy.

Spleen
To perform a spleen protection pyramid, sit comfortably. Draw a large triangle just below your left armpit toward your navel then around your waist, to the opposite point near your spine using

green aventurine. Finally, bring the crystal back to where you have started. Visualize the triangle you have drawn surrounding your spleen as a pyramid. Now, at about a hand's width beneath the armpit, put the green aventurine for about 20 minutes to renew and heal the spleen.

Car

A smoky quartz crystal can be programmed and placed in your car to keep it and you safe at all times. Hold the smoky quartz in your hands while visualizing it surrounded by light. Ask it to protect you, your passengers, and your car all the time. You can also use black tourmaline and program that for protection in your car, to absorb and deflect negative energy. Rose quartz can also help keep passengers and other drivers happy and peaceful. It will keep road rage at bay too. If you have any of these crystals with a point in it, face the point outward to ensure a circle of protection around and inside the car. Amethyst can also be used for its protective and calming qualities. Since cars travel and different passengers can come and go, it is wise to cleanse and rejuvenate any crystals used in your car for protection. It will help to keep them positively charged and vibrating healthily to clear and cleanse them on a regular basis.

Home

Crystals are brilliant and beautiful objects which cannot just beautify your home but also have a very useful holistic purpose. Crystals can assist in keeping the home vibrations and energy vibrant and harmonious. They have the ability to protect your home against electromagnetic pollutions or environmental pollution such as those from microwaves, radio waves, radar, and cellular devices. They can also protect against noisy neighbors. It is important to regularly cleanse the crystals in your home.

Amethyst is one of the super protector stones. It brings a high spiritual vibration into your home. It also guards against psychic attack and negativity, environmental pollution, and ill-wishing. Bloodstone usually works on the physical body, but it also has a strong ability to block out unwanted influences to the home. Place a bloodstone at each corner of your house to keep you and your home protected.

Orange carnelian kept near the front door will attract an abundance of positive realities to your home. Rose quartz placed near an outside wall facing neighbors will guarantee peace and tranquility from them and bring harmony to both homes. It is particularly useful if you have noisy, inconsiderate neighbors as it promotes consideration for others and encourages them to be quiet and peaceful. Rose quartz is a beautiful stone that will always clear negative energy while replacing it with love.

Smoky quartz is a good stone to dispel negative energy from electrical wires, phone towers, nuclear power sources, smog, and x-rays. It is also a good stone to have around if anyone in the house is experiencing depression or has a negative attitude. It will absorb the negativity and emit higher frequency vibes.

Sodalite absorbs the discharge of high-frequency communication antennas, infrared, microwaves, and radar. It also blocks out subtle emanations from your home computer or excessive static electricity. Place sodalite in any room that needs negativity absorbed.

Work
Crystals can be subtle tools for enhancing your workplace and for enabling peaceful coexistence among colleagues. Place one on your desk as a paperweight, on plants, on a windowsill or floor, or on desktop or laptop. Small crystals are as powerful as those larger ones. The whole room can be energized by a small orange carnelian.

Blue lace agate efficiently restores peace and harmony if there is conflict within your working environment. Green aventurine promotes sympathetic leadership and is effective at absorbing environmental pollution and for creating prosperity. It defuses negative situations and turns them into something positive. You can place green aventurine at each corner of your desk or in the desk drawers if you have a co-worker who steals your energy. Labradorite, orange carnelian, smoky quartz, and sodalite are all other good crystals to energize a workplace. Orange carnelian helps to get things done as quickly as possible while being as successful as possible. Smoky quartz can help protect against other's stress and frustration. It also lifts communication problems. You can keep one near your work phone. Sodalite is especially helpful in keeping a group of dynamic people working harmoniously. It creates a basis of trust and solidarity of purpose. Sodalite has the ability to bring things into the open in a non-judgmental manner which can be useful in any workplace.

Electrical equipment has subtle discharges which may really affect your aura surrounding the body. Cell phones, handheld devices, and laptops all create gaps within the biomagnetic sheath around the head and neck and lower chakras. You can place or tape a green aventurine to your phone, computer, or device to block the harmful emanations and revitalize your aura with this crystal. It is an excellent neutralizing stone for all electromagnetic pollution sources. Amethyst, bloodstone, clear quartz, red jasper, rose quartz, green aventurine, smoky quartz, sodalite, and yellow jasper all help block environmental and electromagnetic stress. You can place any of these crystals on the equipment or wear one around your neck.

Strengthening Your Aura

As discussed earlier, your aura is also known as your etheric body or biomagnetic shield. It is a subtle energy field that surrounds your physical body. It is made up of several layers spread out. The outermost layer relates to the spirit, the next layer the mind, the next to emotion, and the one closest to the physical body relates to the physical level of being. Many believe they can sense or even see auras as a white glow or a swirling rainbow of colors. If there are dark or cloudy patches within an aura, that indicates an imbalance or presence of disease or illness. Keeping your biomagnetic sheath as healthy and balanced as possible is an effective defense against illness and guarantees your wellbeing on all levels.

Clear quartz is the main appropriate crystal for strengthening your aura and smoky quartz for cleansing it and getting rid of negative energies. You can train yourself to feel how far your aura extends and to check for weak spots. An energy intuitive healer can sense the state of others' auras. They will use crystals to help keep it clear and strong.

To clear your aura with added benefit of crystals, sit down quietly in a comfortable position. Place smoky quartz at your feet. Place red jasper beneath you and as close to your perineum as possible. Hold labradorite in your left hand. Close your eyes, breathe gently, focusing your attention into your right hand. Extend your right arm out fully with your palm facing your body, or hold clear quartz in this hand. Move your hand slowly toward your body. At some point, your hand will start to tingle and you will be aware of your subtle energy field. This may take some practice. Note how far this field extends from your body. Move your hand with crystal around to see if you can detect any cold or weak spots. If you do, leave the crystal over that spot for a few moments.

With clear quartz, comb your body from the top of your head, working down the front middle of your body to your feet first, then the outside of your body on each side. Finally, run clear quartz as much as you can down your back. Repeat the combing with the Labradorite in your left hand. Place your clear quartz in front of your solar plexus for a few minutes. This will energize your aura. Remember to cleanse the crystals after use.

CHAPTER 7
Using Crystals For Holistic Living

Crystal Prescriptions and Everyday Use

In the natural healing world, among practitioners and healers, crystals can be "prescribed" for specific healing purposes. They can relate to a particular condition or moreover, issues that can very often be perceived as being true. If we work toward correcting an issue, we can reach a state of homeostasis or balance. This allows us to be balanced on all levels, emotional, physical, mental, and spiritual. When we are balanced, energy flows unobstructed and we feel well, happy. If we get stuck, whether emotionally, physically, mentally, or spiritually, energy gets stuck and can manifest as discomfort, disease, a state of illness, and we feel unbalanced and unhappy. Crystals can be a powerful tool to overcome such blockages as grief, stress, rejection, etc. Crystal prescriptions can also help in connecting to our higher selves and divinity. This will bring about clarity, a sense of a bigger picture, and calm spirituality.

Crystals do not have to be used only in a strict healing environment such as a treatment room or during any type of session. Their benefits can be enjoyed on a daily basis, in simple everyday actions. They can help dispel negativity or enhance a state of balance. As always, they reiterate that we are spiritual beings on a human journey. Crystals are here to provide us with added physical, emotional, mental, and spiritual support as needed.

In this chapter, you will find crystal prescriptions, as well as exercises to practice using crystals in everyday life situations. They can be used to help alleviate stress, get back to a state of balance on all levels, or to connect to higher realms and divinity for our greater good. We *can* bring spirituality to our daily lives. Crystals certainly help us connect to our higher selves and enhance spirituality.

Rejection, Loss, or Abandonment

Everyone has felt a rejection of some kind sometime throughout life, whether it was a rejection in a personal relationship or from something else such as a job. We make ourselves available by putting ourselves out there. This is especially true today with so much social media. Whenever we do this, we subject ourselves to any type of "rejection." It is going to happen no matter what and will happen over and over. We cannot control it. What we can control is how we handle or react to the rejection. What you do not want to happen is have fear take over so much so that you do not try new things for fear of further rejection. We have no control over whether somebody wants us, likes us, or chooses us, but that doesn't stop it from hurting when rejection does occur. To heal the pain from rejection, you must return to a place of self-love.

Prescription #1: Rose quartz is extremely effective for this. It is the stone for unconditional love and will bring you back to that space. Wear rose quartz jewelry after hurting from the sting of rejection. Visualize unconditional love flowing from the rose quartz throughout your entire body.

Prescription #2: Yellow tiger's eye can help with self-expression, nurturing and self-motivation. Rejection can hit us right at the core. This can affect our solar plexus chakra and self-image or self-worth. Keeping this chakra strong can help to overcome past rejection and keep from feeling pain of any future rejection. When self-worth is strong, you are less likely to feel pain and loss when you are rejected. To utilize yellow tiger's eye, place the crystal on your solar plexus region while lying down comfortably on your back. Visualize its energy flowing through you and strengthening your sense of self-worth.

Prescription #3: Hematite is a wonderful grounding stone that can help with feelings of safety and security. Overcoming fear of rejection has to do with overcoming fear in general. Fear is an emotion that originates at the root chakra, relating to safety and security. Meditate with a hematite crystal in your receiving, non-dominant hand. Repeat the mantra, "Even when I am afraid, I take risks that serve my highest and greatest good." As you do this, visualize your fear of rejection as a black cloud flowing from your body and into the hematite stone. Cleanse the hematite after the meditation.

Courage

Courage is not about not being afraid. It is about doing what you know to be the right thing for you even though you are afraid. Courage is a trait that originates from the solar plexus chakra, so this is where to focus on crystal use.

Prescription #1: Use citrine as an amplifying crystal with its golden yellow coloring vibrating at the frequency of the solar plexus chakra. In these ways, citrine is a powerful stone of courage. When you feel you need courage, hold a piece of citrine in your receiving or non-dominant hand. Repeat the mantra, "I have the courage to do what I know serves my highest and greatest good."

Prescription #2: Aquamarine is known as one of the stones of courage, so it is a wonderful crystal to carry with you or wear as jewelry when you feel you need a boost of courage. When you know you are going to have to do something out of your comfort zone, adorn yourself with an aquamarine bracelet, necklace, or ring. Call on its energy to bring you courage. Repeat the above mantra. Be grateful for the support of courage. You can also create a courage grid described in the grids section of this book.

Happiness

Happiness is definitely a choice. Sometimes though, when we get overwhelmed by the stress and repetitiveness of our day to day lives, we forget that in order to create happiness or joy, we only have to choose it! The following crystal prescriptions can help you remember to choose happiness regardless of the external situations of your life.

Prescription #1: Amber can be the ultimate stone for happiness. It has a beautiful golden color and a natural warmth that radiates when next to your skin. Wearing amber jewelry can help you vibrate with this happiness energy. It can also serve as a visual reminder to choose to be happy. This can be a life game changer, to follow this advice each day. Hold the amber jewelry in your receiving, non-dominant hand, repeating the mantra, "I choose joy and happiness in every moment!" before putting it on.

Prescription #2: Smoky quartz is a beautiful crystal for transmuting negative energy into positive energy. If you are going through a difficult or stressful time finding it difficult to feel happy, meditate while holding a piece of smoky quartz in each hand. Visualize your negative emotions flowing through your body and into your giving or dominant hand, and into the quartz you are holding. See the quartz change the negative emotion to happiness. Visualize the happiness flowing from the quartz in your giving, dominant hand into the quartz in your receiving, non-dominant hand, up to your arm into your heart, which then pumps it throughout your entire body and being. Feel and delight in pure joy.

Prescription #3: Use citrine to help you be one who spreads happiness and cheer! Before you interact with others, hold a piece of citrine in your giving, dominant hand and repeat the mantra, "Wherever I go and whomever I encounter, I spread happiness." Place the crystal in a pocket and go out into the world. You can also charge small pieces of citrine in this manner and give them to people as gifts, to bring happiness to others.

Inner Peace
All peace, whether it's personal peace, peace within relationships, peace within societies, or world peace, start with inner peace. By being calm no matter what storm is raging outside, you set the vibrational example for others. As others find peace through your example, they spread it as well. It is possible to be in this place of peace, even when the world seems at its darkest. Retreating to your peaceful place can help you weather even the most difficult times.

Prescription #1: Larimar, with its dreamy blue exterior, is a beautiful stone of peace and calm. Use larimar as a gazing crystal. Set it about a foot away from your eyes and gaze at it as you repeat the mantra, "Regardless of what it is happening around me, I am at peace."

Prescription #2: Blue calcite is another peaceful stone. It can help bring you peace even in the most stressful times such as when adrenaline peaks and you experience the fight or flight response. Keep a piece of blue calcite with you and hold it in your receiving, non-dominant hand when you need peace. Visualize the calm blue energy going into your hand through the crystal and flowing throughout your entire body.

Love
We all have love in our lives even when we do not realize it. We are all unconditionally loved by the Divine, Spirit, Universe. Sometimes we feel lonely if our romantic situation is not ideal or we do not have a partner to share in things with. When we experience relationship problems, we fear we may lose love. This is never the case as we are never without love. Like happiness, we must choose to feel love.

Prescription #1: Rose quartz is one of the most common crystals to use for all kinds of unconditional love. If you are seeking romantic love or partnership, meditate with a rose quartz held against your heart chakra. Visualize the energy of love coming out from your heart, passing through the crystal, and expanding into the universe in a way that is magnetic and will attract love. As you do, repeat the mantra, "As I give love to others, so do I receive love in gratitude."

Prescription #2: If you are experiencing difficulty within any type of relationship, peridot can be a very useful crystal to release anger and hurt feelings. It brings loving, healing energy to the relationship. Lie comfortably with a peridot at your heart chakra. Visualize the person with whom you are experiencing difficulty. See a green light extending from your heart, through the peridot, and into the heart of the other person in the relationship you are trying to heal. Repeat this mantra, "I allow love to heal the pain we have caused one another."

Prescription #3: If you feel a lack of trust in a relationship you are in, and that is causing a blockage to love, try working with pink tourmaline which can help build trust. Hold the tourmaline in your giving, dominant hand. Visualize its energy surrounding both of you and feel the love.

Self-Confidence
A lot of issues are caused by not having confidence and low self-esteem. It can be hard to balance the energies of having enough self-confidence to succeed and having too much or too little to either be arrogant or feel unworthy of deserving accomplishments.

It can help to think of a mantra such as "I accept myself unconditionally."

Prescription #1: Yellow tiger's eye again is helpful in building self-confidence while absorbing any excess that could cause self-centeredness or arrogance. Meditate while holding a piece of yellow tiger's eye to your solar plexus region with your giving or dominant hand. Repeat the mantra "I accept myself exactly as I am."

Prescription #2: Citrine is a brilliant crystal that amplifies and strengthens the solar plexus chakra, thus self-confidence and self-worth. Hold citrine in your receiving or non-dominant hand as you meditate while speaking the mantra. Visualize the golden light from the citrine surrounding you completely and flowing through you as self-confidence. Be forgiving and accepting of yourself just as you are. You are completely perfect and worthy of success and happiness no matter what others perceive.

Prescription #3: Amber supports solar plexus chakra energies and projects its own confident warmth. Wear amber jewelry to help keep energies of self-confidence balanced. Wearing a necklace or bracelet is the perfect location for the amber. Amber helps in feelings of security and belonging. It will open you up to accepting yourself for who you are and feel safe in your own self.

Trust
Trust occurs only with feelings of safety and security. Many people struggle with trust issues. Something from our childhood can bring back feelings of mistrust. Those who have experienced mild or significant physical, emotional and mental traumas struggle with trust occasionally. Some struggle on a daily basis. It is necessary to recognize the ways in which we are safe and secure, in order to establish feelings of trust once again. Crystals can be very helpful with this. A mantra to say is "I trust in the compassion and generosity of the universe. I am safe."

Prescription #1: Garnet is a good crystal choice to help establish and keep balanced root chakra energies. These aid in keeping us grounded, feeling safe, and secure. Sit or lie comfortably and place the garnet near your root chakra. Close your eyes if that feels safe to you. Breathe deeply and repeat the mantra above.

Prescription #2: Many of us can lack trust in ourselves. We break our own promises and that can lead to a lack of trust of self. Lack of integrity is a sacral chakra issue. Carnelian is a wonderful crystal choice to balance this chakra. Lie comfortably and place the carnelian on your sacral chakra area. Repeat the mantra "I trust myself because I keep my word to myself."

Prescription #3: Many people feel they cannot trust the world or the universe even. They may feel life, in general, is unsafe and act and react according to this. To help with this, amethyst is a good crystal to help with connecting to higher self and divinity. Listening to Divine guidance leads to greater trust in the universe. Place an amethyst on your third eye chakra. Meditate as you repeat the mantra above.

Relieve stress
Stress can show up as physical, mental, or even emotional and really affects the human body. When you are stressed, especially chronically, the adrenal glands that are located above the kidneys go into "fight or flight" mode, causing an overproduction of adrenaline in the body. This increases cortisol and causes your body to react in multiple negative ways. Symptoms of stress include headaches, bloating, aches and pains, depression, fatigue, restlessness, ulcers, and even auto-immune diseases just to name a few. If excess adrenaline and cortisol are not removed from your body, it can feel impossible to relax or sleep. Lying or sitting quietly for 20 minutes helps to release stress with an appropriate crystal. Also, you can wear and carry one whenever you feel the need to relax and recharge.

These gems may also provide great assistance when you are suffering from any number of forms of stress. In today's fast-paced, electronic-based world, it is no wonder stress, which can lead to anxiety, is one of the most common discomforts people complain about. Managing stress is essential for overall health and balance. Gratefully, crystals can help.

Crystals to Use for Relieving Stress

Green Aventurine and Rose Quartz are both good at helping to prevent over-production of adrenaline and reduce the feeling of restlessness. Green aventurine helps mental stress and rose quartz aids in emotional stress, but they both work together to support each other and enhance their effectiveness. Place or tape rose quartz on your left kidney and green aventurine on your right kidney, just above your waist and on either side of your spine. Leave on for about 20 minutes to significantly reduce adrenaline over-production.

Amethyst is a wonderful crystal to use if you are feeling stressed, especially if experiencing tension headaches. Put the amethyst on the center of your forehead or at the back of your skull and lie still, counting to six while breathing in slowly. Hold your breath for six seconds and then breath out for seven seconds. Do this for fifteen to twenty minutes to feel completely relaxed. Amethyst can be extremely calming. It attracts positive energy while getting rid of negative energy. When you are feeling especially stressed out, you may try placing it under your pillow at night.

Bloodstone is an excellent stone to keep your mind calm and focused during times of mental stress, supporting the immune system as well.

Clear quartz and labradorite are both good stones to help you maneuver through emotional stress. Labradorite will gently bring up suppressed emotions that may be contributing to disease. Clear quartz will energize and recharge if stress is causing you to feel exhausted.

Rose quartz is a calming stone that supports during emotional trauma, giving you reassurance and helping you to accept necessary change. It lends itself to feelings of unconditional love which can help relieve stress.

Smoky quartz helps relieve stress, especially if caused by harmful environmental energies. It is also a very stabilizing stone. It can help you regain balance after being thrown into fight or flight mode due to stress. It helps to keep you calm under overwhelming situations and protects against environmental stress. Keep smoky quartz with you whenever you feel stressed or anxious. Hold it while breathing in and out slowly, until you feel calm and stable.

Yellow Jasper is an excellent crystal if you feel you need support or nurturing during stressful times. It brings about tranquility and can give you the added strength to overcome difficulties.

Anxiety
Anxiety can be an occasional thing such as common worrying, or it can be a chronic or even debilitating condition. If left untreated, stress and anxiety can lead to a whole host of other diseases including heart disease. There are many types of anxiety such as social anxiety, phobias, obsessive-compulsive disorders, and general anxiety. The prescriptions here are for persistent anxiety as opposed to short-term stress, which is covered in other prescriptions. Anxiety is a condition of excessive energy, so you should work with opaque stones that absorb, soothe, and calm.

Prescription #1: Amber can help support you when you are feeling anxious. For social anxiety, wear amber as a necklace, bracelet, or ring, or carry a piece carefully wrapped, in a pocket as you go into socially intense situations. In these situations, amber will help ease your anxiety. Hold a piece of amber in your receiving, non-dominant hand and note the warmth of it. Visualize a yellow light connection from your solar plexus to the solar plexus of other people in the room. Breathe deeply as long as you need, until the anxiety passes.

Prescription #2: Sodalite has a calming blue color and can be seen as the perfect anti-anxiety crystal. It balances energies while connecting to intuition and spirituality. Hold a piece of sodalite in your giving, dominant hand. Sit calmly and relaxed. Close your eyes if that feels safe to you. Visualize your anxiety flowing through you into your dominant arm, into your hand, and into the sodalite. As you visualize, repeat the mantra, "I am peace." Do this at least once a day and cleanse the sodalite daily.

Prescription #3: Anxiety is common in the evening when we are trying to rest or go to sleep. When our bodies are ready for sleep, our mind can go into overdrive and cause anxiety-induced insomnia. If your anxiety arises when trying to sleep, try this two-part remedy. Add four to five drops of lavender essential oil in a bathtub filled with warm water. If it is warmer months and you have it, place actual lavender stems and leaves from the plant. Soak for ten to twelve minutes. As you lie still and your anxieties rise to the top, watch them drift away and repeat the mantra or word, "calm." Sit in the tub as it drains and visualize your worries draining with the water. When the water is completely drained and your anxieties with it, get out and gently dry off. Then crawl into bed with a piece of amethyst taped underneath the head of your bed or on your bedside table or both. Again, as anxieties arise, visualize them as clouds that drift harmlessly out of your head and into the universe. Repeat the mantra or any calming phrase you resonate with.

Balance

When we are out of balance in any way, it can make it seem like our whole life is spiraling out of control. Lack of balance manifests in many ways, such as poor work to life balance, excessive focus on body, mind, or spirit at the expense of others, or too much stress without enough relaxation just to name a few. The first step is recognizing you are out of balance in some way. Next, you can use these prescriptions and the healing power of crystals as you seek to get back to a state of balance or homeostasis.

Prescription #1: Rainbow fluorite with its large array of colors can help balance energies. Wear rainbow fluorite as jewelry when you feel out of balance. It will help balance and stabilize all energies and aid in connecting mind, body, and spirit. It is a very harmonizing crystal. A few times a day, especially upon waking and when going to bed, hold a piece of fluorite in your receiving or non-dominant hand, and repeat the mantra, "I am balanced in all things."

Prescription #2: Use turquoise as a stone of harmony that can help balance your energies and bring you back to a centered place of calm peace. Wear turquoise jewelry as a great way to enjoy this crystal as you seek balance. Be sure to clear the turquoise every few days to retain its harmonic power.

Prescription #3: Black tourmaline and clear quartz work in harmony to create balanced energy throughout your system. They are grounding, cleansing, and overall healing stones. Lie on the floor or on a comfortable bed or sofa. Place a piece of black tourmaline near your root chakra and a piece of quartz near your crown chakra. Close your eyes if this feels safe to you. Visualize energy flowing from root to crown and back. Repeat the mantra if it feels right. Feel the working healing energy bringing you back to complete balance.

Boundaries

Creating and keeping healthy boundaries is something many people have difficulty with. Maintaining these boundaries, however, is essential for mental, spiritual, emotional, and physical health. Having firm boundaries in place protects your sense of self while still allowing you to interact with others in ways that are kind and compassionate, both to you and to another. Boundaries shouldn't be so strict that they do not allow for loving action when it is required. Therefore, they need to be firm but flexible, and ultimately, self-loving.

Prescription #1: Yellow kyanite has two properties that make it a great stone for setting boundaries. First, it's a part of the triclinic crystal system, which is a boundary or perimeter stone. Second, it supports the solar plexus chakra, which is where the energy of a healthy sense of self and boundaries exists. As you meditate, hold a piece of yellow kyanite in your giving, or dominant hand and repeat the mantra, "My boundaries are firm but flexible enough to allow for love." Do this for five to ten minutes, or until you feel your boundaries are firmly in place.

Prescription #2: Turquoise, another triclinic crystal, is an excellent boundary setter. Wearing turquoise jewelry of any kind is strongly recommended. Put a piece of turquoise jewelry on in the morning. Repeat the mantra, "My boundaries are firm but flexible enough to allow for love," as you visualize energy expanding from the turquoise and surrounding you.

Prescription #3: Labradorite helps you find empowerment and connects you to your intuition, which helps you have the strength to set healthy boundaries. It is also a stone associated with the throat chakra, which can help you speak your own truth, something necessary for giving voice to your boundaries. When someone asks you to do something, take a moment and pause. Hold a piece of labradorite in your hand and ask yourself, "Is this something that is within my own personal boundaries to do?" See what answer comes to you. It is okay to say no if you feel it is beyond your personal boundaries.

Compassion

Compassion, whether for ourselves or others, is one of the most important qualities you can foster. Sometimes it can be difficult to feel compassion, including self-compassion. It is an essential high vibration quality that allows us to experience ourselves and others, as Divine.

Prescription #1: Compassion is an emotion that comes from your spirit and from your heart. Because the desire is to amplify compassion, using an amplifying crystal can help you grow and nurture this important quality. Rose quartz is one of the highest vibrational stones for cultivating compassion and as a hexagonal system stone, it is also a natural amplifier. For self-compassion, hold the rose quartz stone in your receiving or non-dominant hand and hold it at your heart. For compassion for others, hold the rose quartz in your giving or dominant hand and hold it at your heart. Close your eyes if that is comfortable for you. Repeat the mantra, "Everything and everyone I see before me, I see with compassionate eyes." Feel compassion moving through you.

Prescription #2: Sometimes it can be difficult to experience compassion until you release judgment. Aquamarine is another hexagonal, amplifying stone that can help you let go. When you notice that judgment about yourself or another is blocking compassion, hold the aquamarine in your giving or dominant hand and visualize releasing judgment. As you hold the stone, repeat this mantra, "I release judgment. I allow compassion."

Prescription #3: Peridot is another crystal of the heart, a stone of compassion. Its bright green clarity can help in promoting healing of the heart to feel compassion regularly. It will also help with letting go in order to make room for compassion and love of all types. Lie comfortably on your back and place a peridot on your heart chakra. Notice the beating of your heart. Close your eyes if that feels safe to you. Visualize someone or something for whom you have tremendous compassion for. Pull that feeling of love and compassion into your heart and feel it filling your body with every beat of your heart, moving through all your blood vessels into every part of your body. Feel love and compassion expanding beyond you and into the world, out into the universe even. Do this for as long as you feel comfortable and like.

Crystals for Your Spirit and Connecting with Divinity

Crystals are full of spiritual energy and light as earth elements, vibrating brilliantly and strongly. They can definitely provide support to the spirit in opening intuition. Quartzes and labradorite are high-vibration crystals that work to ground spiritual energy into the physical body. They also provide great insight.

Hold one of the following five intuition crystals at your third eye whenever you need spiritual guidance or support.

Labradorite works in two ways to enhance intuition. First, it brings messages from the unconscious mind to the surface and helps to intuitively understand them. Second, it accesses other lives and other realms, bringing intuitive wisdom to the forefront. Labradorite is especially useful to get to the heart of matters and to understand the actual motivation behind other people's thoughts and actions.

Sodalite unites logic with intuition. It initiates spiritual awareness and brings information from the higher mind to the everyday mind. This stone stimulates the pineal gland, directly correlated to your third eye and third eye chakra, thus deepens spiritual perception.

Clear quartz can behave like a database. It stores information and is a spiritual library just waiting to be accessed. This stone enhances intuition and psychic abilities. It has been used since the beginning of time as a scrying stone to transport into the future or past.

Amethyst is one of the great heighteners of intuition and spiritual awareness. The calming energies of amethyst take you to a different plane. It is an excellent crystal for gazing into as a scrying tool and can be placed on the third eye to access it.

Smoky quartz brings higher spiritual energies down to earth. It can be used as scrying stone to initiate intuition and stay focused in it. This can be achieved by holding the smoky quartz and gaze into its depths, allowing your eyes to go out of focus. This is very similar to meditation. Notice what comes into your mind. Don't judge it and just let it go.

Connecting with the Divine
Connecting to Divine energies and the spiritual realm often happens when meditating. With the assistance of crystals, you can be connected to Divine energy all of the time. Consciously connecting to Divine energy and then directing it into your crystal allows you to always be linked to Divine universal light.

Labradorite again comes into play when raising spiritual vibration and connecting to divinity. It is a highly mystical stone, raising your consciousness to the highest possible level so that you can make contact with the Divine. It then connects the energies into your body and grounds it there. It takes esoteric knowledge to nourish your soul.

Rose quartz is the stone of unconditional love. It takes you into the heart of the Divine light. It helps you realize that you are a spiritual being whose true being is Divine. This enhances overall spiritual awareness.

Blue lace agate is a spiritually uplifting stone. It can take you on a cosmic journey to your Divine home. It can help to place under your pillow or near your bed while sleeping, to travel in your dream state.

Clear quartz carries the vibration of Divine light. Just by holding clear quartz above your head for a few minutes, you can experience a flood of spiritual energy that connects you directly with the Divine.

Travel spiritual waves
Holding blue lace agate, be aware of the gentle arcs that flow over its surface. These are the waves in the sea of spirit to which all beings belong. Trace these curves with your eyes, letting them go a

little out of focus. Travel the waves until you reach your spiritual home. Bring the stone to your throat and anchor the connection there.

Anchoring divine light
Holding labradorite and gazing into its depths, be aware that the blue flashes you see are the light of the Divine anchored into your crystal. Know that whenever you hold this crystal, you will have an immediate connection to the Divine. Place this crystal to your forehead and absorb the diving light into your whole being.

Attuning to unconditional love
Holding rose quartz, allow yourself to feel the unconditional love radiating out from its serene center. This is the love that is at the heart of the universe and which moves through all things. Place the stone over your heart and allow your heart to absorb this unconditional, Divine love, feeling it rush through your whole being.

Crystal programming
Crystals are programmable. They will still work even if not programmed, but when they are, it is like bringing a laser beam focus to them. It sets a clear intention for a very specific purpose, a need, or desire. The crystal will then help in any way they can to achieve this intention. They will be super focused. It is best to program a crystal to go along with their natural properties. Program a stress relieving crystal to help alleviate stress. Program a crystal that helps with digestion to aid in digestive issues. To do this, for a few moments, hold your crystal in your hands, imagining that it is surrounded by light. Affirm the intention that should be brought to you by the crystal. Again, only if you are comfortable in doing so, you may program your crystals. It can make them even more focused and powerful, but they will not lose any qualities by not programming.

Healing dreams
You can program your crystal to help aid in healing dreams. Hold your stone of choice in your hands and imagine it bathed in white, healing light. State your intention that your crystal will bring you a healing dream that you will remember and understand when you awaken. Then place the crystal under your pillow before you go to

sleep. Keep a pen and paper or a dream journal by your bed to write down your dream.

Some helpful crystals for dreaming are red and yellow jasper. They assist in recalling significant dreams. Jasper helps the subconscious mind to communicate with the conscious mind in the dream state. Bloodstone stimulates vivid dreaming. Amethyst makes intuitive dreams and journeys out of the body easier and helps you in understanding your dreams. An amethyst under your pillow protects against nightmares and ensures sweet dreams.

Dream Healer
A simple yet effective visualization before going to sleep can put you in contact with the dream healer. Begin by sitting or lying down comfortably. Holding an amethyst in your hands to enhance your visualization abilities, rest quietly and close your eyes. Breathe slowly and evenly, focusing your attention deep within yourself. Without opening your eyes, raise them to be looking at your third eye in the center of your forehead. Imagine this eye-opening and revealing a peaceful, beautiful place in which you can enter into. If this is especially hard at first, place the amethyst on your third eye to stimulate its opening.

Spend a few moments going around in and enjoying this beautiful place, however it is you are picturing it. There is no right or wrong type of place. As you explore, you will become aware of a figure joining you. This figure is the dream healer. It is not necessarily human. Explain to the dream healer exactly what kind of healing you need, whether it is physical, emotional, mental, or spiritual. If you do not know the source of your disease, then ask the dream healer to assess and give the correct type of healing. Request that tonight, you will receive healing, and that upon waking, you will recall your dream clearly and know exactly what it means.

When you go to bed, place your amethyst under your pillow. Confirm to yourself that you will be meeting the dream healer and that you will remember your dream. When you wake up, write the dream and any thoughts on it in your dream journal.

Crystal meditation

Meditation is anything that focuses your mind on the present moment. A mantra is any word or phrase that focuses you on an intention or affirmation. Together with the use of powerful yet subtle crystal power, meditation can transform and heal. Meditation is one of the simplest ways to connect with the healing power of crystals. Each crystal will feel different so keep experimenting and be grateful and patient.

Meditation rests an overactive mind and puts you in touch with your spirituality. It can greatly turn off the "fight or flight" response you may be experiencing from stress or anxiety. Gazing into the center of a clear crystal enables you to quickly enter a meditative state. Crystals have a natural likeness to meditation as they calm your mind and allow it to be open to receive spiritual energy. Your brain waves change according to levels of consciousness. When we are in an altered state of higher consciousness such as during meditation, our alpha brain waves are dominant. During everyday awareness, we emit beta brain waves. Holding a smoky quartz crystal can help move between beta brain waves and alpha brain waves. Smoky quartz is also a calming of the mind crystal. It is an excellent stone choice for meditation.

Sodalite is useful to activate higher awareness and stimulates spirituality, allowing meditation to go to a deeper level.

Crystals and meditation go hand in hand. There is a ritual you can perform to help meditate using crystals. Settle yourself in a quiet, peaceful area where you know you will not be disturbed. Focus on your breathing gently and evenly. As you inhale, imagine great peace and allow your body to relax and soften. As you exhale, let go of any tension or thoughts and anxieties. Allow your body and your mind to settle into a still place. Using your crystal toolkit, but not yet using labradorite, make a crystal chakra circle around yourself starting at the brown of smoky quartz through red, orange, and yellow to green and blue, then into purple amethyst and clear quartz. Focus on each crystal for a few moments before touching it to your third eye and then placing it back in the circle.

Hold labradorite in your hands and turn it until it catches the light, to then gaze into its enigmatic depths. Breathe more deeply, into your belly, consciously grounding yourself with spiritual energy.

Close your eyes. Allow all thoughts or sounds to drift right past you and be aware only of the crystal in your hands, its energy, and the insight it brings to you.

After 10 to 20 minutes, gather up your crystals and place them to one side. Holding smoky quartz, stand up and feel your feet firmly on the ground. Be mindful of the grounding cord that goes from your feet deep into the earth to hold you gently in your physical body. Be grateful for your spiritual being in human experience. Thank your higher self and any spiritual energy felt during meditating.

Protection against electromagnetic field or EMF
All electronics emit an electromagnetic field. We are bombarded by electronics with widespread cell phone use, handheld devices, laptops, computers, speakers, microwaves, etc. These emissions cause negative effects on our physical, emotional, and mental wellbeing. Crystals help dispel these negative forces. A powerful shield against EMF is the crystal Shungite. It helps to absorb negative pollutants, toxins, and energy. It is a very powerful crystal with strong effects on the body. It can soothe anxiety and increase the detoxification process. Try placing shungite near your computer or wi-fi hub while you work, on your cell phone, or you can wear the crystal to shield you.

Cultivate love and revitalize your sex life
Rose quartz is a stone of unconditional love as mentioned many times here. This beautiful gem revitalizes and heals the energy of the heart and heart chakra. It emanates love and compassion vibrations. It is nurturing as well as supportive while giving a person to feel the most potent energy of the universe — love! It will encourage you to practice more self-love and will also bring love. Many healers will say this is the secret to finding true love. Rose quartz can help heal old wounds to forgive past loves while releasing any lingering negative emotions. If you are single and looking for a compatible, loving mate, near your bedside or wherever you spend a lot of time in a relaxed state, you may place two rose quartz crystals.

Sexuality and sexual activity is linked to the lower chakras. When these chakras are clear and working properly, libido is able to flow freely. Crystals energize these points as well as those of the emotional body so love can be given and received without restraint. Your sex life can be regenerated if you and your partner utilize some of these lower chakra enhancing crystals.

Red Jasper is an excellent crystal for stimulating your libido and prolonging sexual pleasure. This stone cleanses and energizes the base or root chakra. Orange carnelian is a recharging crystal. It energizes the sacral chakra, helps to overcome impotence or low libido, and restores vitality to the female reproductive organs. Smoky quartz helps you to accept that you are in a physical body with normal and natural sexual desires. It clears the lower chakras so that your passion can flow unobstructed. Rose quartz opens your heart chakra and restores love and trust between you and your partner. It enables you to love yourself in order to receive love from someone else. This stone also increases fertility.

Activating and care of crystals
In order for crystals to work for you, they must be cleansed, activated, and attuned to your particular frequency. This helps to get rid of any vibrations they may have picked up on before getting to you. Crystals should be cleared and cleansed often, especially after a healing session.

Clearing or cleansing of crystals
There are a few ways to clear crystals. One of them is to keep them under running water for a few minutes, to then place them in the sun for a few hours. If the sun is not out, envision a white light that radiates down in your crystals. You can also place crystal quartz near any other crystal you wish to clear. You may burn sage or a smudge-stick around the crystals you wish to clear. Even burying crystals in the earth or placing in the moonlight will clear a crystal appropriately. You can also use sound. The vibrations of a pure sound such as a bell, gong, tuning fork, or singing bowl can be used to energetically clean a crystal. It is always important to cleanse your crystals before and after a healing session.

To activate your crystals, hold them in your hands. With your eyes shut, concentrate on the crystals and see them surrounded by healing, white light. Ask that they be attuned to your own unique frequency and that they will be activated to act as healers at any level you may need now or anytime in the future. Ask that the crystals be blessed by the highest energies in the universe and be dedicated to your self-healing and the environment around you.

The best way to store your healing stones is individually wrapped in a cloth bag. A plastic bin with individual compartments as used for beads or crafts can be used for smaller crystals. If they are kept out in the daily environment, they can and will absorb negative energy and need to be cleansed or cleared more often. You should also keep crystals and stones dust and dirt free by wiping them with only a soft cloth. You can also wear stones or keep them in your pocket until ready to use.

Practical use of crystals
You can use crystals in so many ways as described here in this book. Healing sessions and meditation are two very common methods, but others exist as well. There are suggestions in the specific crystals and conditions sections of this book so you will know how to use them, but the tips below are very practical suggestions for applied use.

Crystal elixirs - Place clean, cleared crystals in a bowl of spring or purified water in the sunshine for two hours. Remove the crystals then and drink the water as needed. You can also create a crystal spray by placing crystals in spring or purified water, again with a specific intent for the crystal. Keep it in the sun or moonlight for up to five hours or even overnight. Remove the crystals, place the charged water in a darkened spray bottle with about a teaspoon of brandy or vinegar as a preservative. Spritz the spray as needed, on or around yourself, your home, your car, pets, etc.

Secure a piece of fluorite to the bottom of your work chair to help you stay focused.

Carry carnelian in a pants pocket or wear it as a bracelet when you need a boost of creativity.

Wear rose quartz so it hangs over your heart center when you are expecting or involved in a romantic activity.

Drop water safe crystals in your bathwater. Remove them before draining the tub.

Wear happy and energetic amber to give you a positive boost.

Sprinkle positive energy crystals such as smoky quartz or crystals that absorb negative energy such as black tourmaline, around the perimeter of your house to keep negativity at bay. You can use inexpensive crystal chips or beads for this.

Sacred Space
Sacred spaces are peaceful, welcoming environments that create a clean, free-flowing energy space. They are often seen in yoga and meditation practices or studios. They can also be seen in a practitioner's offices such as a chiropractor, massage therapist, or energy worker. You can create an altar or sacred space in your home. Using crystals in these calming spaces adds a beautiful piece of earth energy surrounded by peace, unconditional love, and acceptance. The addition and use of crystals in a sacred space can serve as a reminder to reconnect with your intention each time you revisit the space.

Amethyst is a very useful, popular crystal for sacred spaces. It emits positive energy and nurtures a deeper state of meditation and connecting to your higher self and divinity. Crystal points can also help set an intention in your space, especially on or near an altar. Write your intention on a piece of paper and place a crystal point on top of it. The point amplifies the intention into the universe.

Carry crystals
Once you set an intention or program a crystal, you can carry it with you to remind yourself of that intention. The more direct contact you have with a crystal, the more aware you'll be of its energy. You will be able to easily access it whenever you need to feel grounded, center yourself or bring your attention back to the intention you are working toward.

Crystals and yoga
Placing crystals on your yoga mat can increase the power of asanas and any intention set forth during meditation during your practice.

You can even place crystals on your body during yoga to encourage a deeper state of healing.

Home décor
Crystals large and small help to add to home décor beauty. They can help achieve positive feng shui and dispel negative energy while emitting positive vibes. They look beautiful and like pieces of art as well. They can be a perfect addition to any room while serving a specific purpose. The placement of crystals in areas of the home was discussed earlier. So while beautifying a space, they can also be powerful catalysts for positive energy in your home.

Home spa treatment
Placing crystals in and around your home, self-care treatments can enhance healing and add a calming aspect to your routine. Place only strong crystals able to withstand warm water into your bath or around your shower or bathtub. You can soak with the crystals in a bath or hot tub or in water in the sink you plan to wash your face with. The crystal energy will have peaceful and restorative effects on your at home spa day. Crystals in your bathroom and any room or area you get ready in at the beginning or end of the day can help you feel relaxed and prepared for that time of the day.

CHAPTER 8
Crystals For Disorders, Specific Ailments, And Systems

In addition to the previously mentioned disorders, diseases, and illnesses, the following specific conditions can benefit from regular crystal therapy. Crystal use never claims to cure any ailment. Crystal therapy is only ever meant to complement any other treatment and never meant to cure nor prescribe. Seek proper medical attention for any illness.

Aches and pains
Aragonite, blue lace agate, celestite, charoite, chrysocolla, clear quartz, lapis lazuli, and malachite all help with relieving general aches and pains.

Addiction
Amethyst is helpful in overcoming addictions or overindulgences of any kind. It has a calming effect.

ADD/ADHD
Fluorite, crystal and lithium quartz, lepidolite, petalite, and stilbite help to balance energies associated with ADD and ADHD.

AIDS/HIV
Carnelian, clear quartz, lapis lazuli, and malachite help in dealing with symptoms of HIV AIDS.

Allergies
Green aventurine, zircon, and aquamarine help with allergies and allergy symptoms.

Alzheimer's
Rose quartz is a good crystal to help reduce the confusion of Alzheimer's and senile dementia.

Anger

Carnelian, amethyst, rose quartz, peridot, and muscovite help with anger issues and to release restricted negativity that causes deep-rooted anger.

Anxiety/Panic Attacks
Sodalite calms anxiety attacks. Keep it in your pocket and hold it over your chest at the first sign of an attack. Breathe slowly and deeply while counting to seven, hold your breath for a count of six, and then exhale for a count of five. Rose quartz can also help relieve anxiety and prevent panic attacks.

Arthritis
Blue lace agate and orange carnelian are useful in easing the pain of arthritis.

Autism
Amethyst, blue lace agate, sodalite, charoite, lapis lazuli, and clear quartz all help with autism imbalances.

Auto-immune Disorders
Aquamarine, red aventurine, carnelian, and turquoise are good for relieving auto-immune disorder symptoms.

Bacterial Infections
Bloodstone is effective in clearing bacterial infections. Place over the thymus gland for optimal results.

Back Pain
Hematite, lapis lazuli, orange carnelian, fluorite, and smoky quartz can help alleviate back pain, including lower back issues.

Bladder Issues
Use bloodstone crystal for clearing of blood, kidneys, and blockages in general and to aid in bladder issues. It also helps to soothe inflammation and irritation in and around the bladder.

Blood Pressure, High
Sodalite, Green Aventurine, bloodstone, and labradorite are helpful to relieve high blood pressure.

Blood Pressure, Low

Rose quartz is a good crystal to help with low blood pressure issues.

Blood Problems
Orange carnelian, red jasper, and bloodstone are useful for blood issues such as anemia.

Bones
Orange carnelian, howlite, and fluorite are all good choices in working with bone issues.

Brain Health
Amethyst, aventurine, Botswana agate, and lapis lazuli help with overall brain health.

Breast Health
Amazonite, lapis lazuli, moonstone, peridot, rainbow moonstone, and milky/snow quartz are all good choice crystals to balance breast and chest health.

Bruises
Amethyst and rose quartz help with healing bruises quickly.

Chemotherapy
Smoky quartz can help clear and alleviate the negative effects of chemotherapy.

Childbirth and Labor Pains
Amethyst, bloodstone, lapis lazuli, and tiger iron help in labor pain and childbirth.

Chronic Fatigue
Carnelian, citrine, chalcedony, Jasper, and tourmaline aid in relieving chronic fatigue syndrome.

Cholesterol
Fluorite and green aventurine help the body rid of the negative effects of high cholesterol.

Circulation
Bloodstone and red jasper help with poor circulation.

Claustrophobia
Green aventurine helps with claustrophobia.

Colds
Bloodstone helps clear blockages associated with the common cold, especially if placed over the thymus gland. Citrine, amber, and aventurine can also help.

Constipation
Malachite, citrine, and apatite help with constipation and digestive issues related to it.

Cramps
Smoky quartz can help relieve all types of cramps.

Depression
Amethyst, orange carnelian, and smoky quartz are good crystals in dealing with depression. Amethyst is a powerful calming stone, orange carnelian can activate a sense of security, and smoky quartz is a gentle yet effective mood enhancer. All of these crystals stabilize your energies enabling them to function harmoniously.

Diabetes
Citrine, red jasper, sodalite, emerald, and malachite all help in aiding diabetes.

Digestion
Sodalite, yellow jasper, citrine, and apatite all aid with digestive issues.

Ear Issues
Amethyst, amber, tourmaline, snowflake obsidian, and clear quartz point all help in dealing with issues related to ears.

Eating Disorders
Citrine, amber, tiger's eye, and yellow jasper are beneficial for those struggling with eating disorders.

Endocrine System
Amethyst helps with endocrine imbalances.

Energy
Orange, red carnelian, and red jasper benefit energy depletion or fatigue.

Eye Issues
Blue lace agate, green aventurine, and labradorite can be helpful with eye problems.

Fever
Hematite, peridot, sodalite, and blue lace agate all help relieve symptoms of fever.

Flu
Bloodstone, carnelian, citrine, amber, and aventurine all help alleviate flu symptoms.

Headache
Selenite, amethyst, quartz, and lapis lazuli are good for headaches, including migraines.

Hormone imbalance
Placing an amethyst over your pituitary gland can help with hormonal imbalance.

Immune System
Blue lace agate, green aventurine, bloodstone, amethyst, amber, and fluorite all aid in immune system disorders.

Insomnia
Amethyst, sodalite, and bloodstone are crystals of choice to alleviate insomnia. Place one or all of these stones under your pillow or near your bed and positively intent or program them to help you sleep well. They will calm and stabilize your body, mind, and spirit for a sound sleep.

Joint Pain and Arthritis
Blue lace agate, apatite, bloodstone, copper, fluorite, and hematite are all excellent at aiding in alleviating inflammation, assists in bone, teeth, and cell regeneration, increasing blood flow and circulation, and absorbing of calcium. Blue lace agate is known to remove blockages within the nervous system that can lead to

physical pain in muscles and joints. Place this healing crystal in your bath water for 15 to 20 minutes.

Learning Challenges
Clear quartz, amethyst, rose quartz, citrine, aventurine, and carnelian help in aiding those struggling with learning challenges.

Leukemia
Bloodstone, peridot, alexandrite, and smoky quartz are helpful for those dealing with leukemia issues.

Lupus
Bloodstone, amber, fluorite, and hematite are all detoxifying, immune system boosting, and healing crystals helpful in relieving negative effects of lupus.

Lymphatic System
Blue lace agate, sodalite, bloodstone, and rose quartz help enhance and clear the lymphatic system.

Menstrual Disorders
Citrine, moonstone, labradorite, and amethyst help in pre and menstrual symptoms.

Metabolic System
Amethyst, sodalite, orange carnelian, bloodstone, and labradorite help to keep the metabolic system in balance.

Mid-life Crisis
Rose quartz is helpful to maneuver through a mid-life crisis, enabling you to get your life back on track.

Neurosis
Green aventurine is beneficial in severe neurosis. It helps to understand the underlying reason behind the condition.

Nervous System
Blue lace agate, rose quartz, and amethyst benefits the nervous system.

Phobias

Sodalite is an excellent crystal choice to help you overcome your phobias. Green aventurine specifically overcomes claustrophobia.

Skeletal System
Blue lace agate, howlite, fluorite, and apatite are all good crystal choices for general bone growth and health. Even lapis lazuli can help strengthen the skeletal structure.

Sleep Disorders
Crystals to help relieve sleep troubles include amethyst, clear quartz, labradorite, rose quartz, black tourmaline, and angelite.

Sore Throat
Amber, aquamarine, blue lace agate, and sodalite help relieve a sore throat.

Stress
Amethyst, clear quartz, moonstone, rose quartz, tourmaline, howlite, sodalite, and labradorite are wonderful crystals to help alleviate all kinds of stress.

Transition
Amethyst, garnet, malachite, labradorite, rose quartz, and clear quartz help aid in transition or change of any kind, including crossing over.

Varicose Veins
Adding bloodstone to bath water can help relieve varicose veins.

Wrinkles
Rose quartz will help increase self-love and get rid of the negative effects of wrinkles.

CONCLUSION

Thank you so much for making it through to the end of this book. I hope it was informative and able to provide you with many of the tools you may need as you begin your Crystal Healing journey. The next step is to try some of the techniques described here, to practice in your own life. Find out what works best for you and what feels right. Remember to keep an open mind. Know that healing can be a slow and steady process. Follow your intuition using information in this book to help you start a useful and meaningful crystal collection. Crystals can be subtle yet powerful. If a particular stone resonates with you when you see or hold it, do not disregard that. It is telling you to listen to what your body, mind, and spirit are saying and that you may need it for support.

You can lead the balanced life you desire, filled with positive energy! It is possible to release unwanted negativity. Let go of what is no longer needed. Forgive yourself and others and behold your true being. Live the life that is meant for You! Crystals and their healing powers can allow you to follow this holistic approach toward your mind, body, and spirit.

Finally, if you enjoyed this book, please take the time to rate it on Amazon. Your honest review would be greatly appreciated. Thank you!

DESCRIPTION

Discover the gentle, non-invasive healing power of crystals! Learn about and use these natural earth element stones that connect us to our higher selves and higher beings, in order to activate our inner healing abilities. *Healing Crystals* will allow you to become knowledgeable in many aspects regarding the healing power of crystals. You will be able to recognize their healing qualities in order to improve all areas of your life holistically, in powerful ways. You will be able to reference this book every day. These are a few of the Crystal Healing techniques you will read about to incorporate into your daily life:

- History, properties, meaning, and purpose of popular healing crystals
- Crystal grids at home, at work, on the go, wherever you are
- Colors of crystals and how they relate to corresponding chakras
- Chakra balancing using crystals for everyday centeredness
- Aura clearing, cleansing, and protecting using crystals
- Using crystals in relaxation, meditation, healing, and positive affirmation
- Crystals as powerful healers — how they aid in specific ailments such as depression, exhaustion, grief, joint pain, and more
- Crystals for balancing the body, mind, and spirit holistically
- Crystals in Reiki — positive intent, connecting to higher self and Divinity for the greater good
- Crystal prescriptions

Crystals can be subtle yet powerful in their healing work. While they may not initiate change overnight, with continual use, keeping an open mind and believing in their healing properties, they can help us overcome emotional blockages that may be causing physical ailments that could last a lifetime. This is the amazing power of crystals. They can quickly alleviate a tension headache but also support us through our life's journeys and soul's lessons. This can result in a long-lasting improvement on any number of conditions and ailments. Crystals can also benefit us in our daily lives to help us cultivate our own courage, true voice, compassion for self and others.

www.ingramcontent.com/pod-product-compliance
Lightning Source LLC
Chambersburg PA
CBHW071505070526
44578CB00001B/451